11+ English
Study and Practice Book

Charlotte Watson

Name _____

Schofield & Sims

Contents

Contents

Introduction

This book will help you to prepare for the English part of your 11+ exam. It will help you improve your English knowledge and practise a range of English skills, focusing on key areas, such as homophones and apostrophes, to help you avoid common mistakes.

The topics are grouped into six sections:

- grammar
- punctuation
- spelling
- vocabulary
- comprehension
- writing.

You might not be tested on all these topics in your 11+ exam, but it is important to revise them in case they do come up.

If you are sitting an 11+ exam set by CEM, the verbal reasoning section of your exam may include some comprehension questions, which are explained in this book. Explanations and examples of other verbal reasoning question types can be found in the **11+ Verbal Reasoning Study and Practice Book**, which is also available from Schofield & Sims.

How to use this book

Before you start using this book, write your name in the box on the first page. Then decide how to begin. If you want a complete course in English, work right through the book. If you want to find out about a particular type of question, use the Contents page or the Index to find the pages you need. Whichever way you choose to use the book, don't try to cover too much at once – it is better to work in short bursts.

Most questions have space to write the answers directly in the book. However, you will need rough paper to answer some questions, particularly in the Comprehension and Writing sections.

As you make a start, look out for the symbols below, which mark different parts of the text. Find out about words in **grey** by turning to the Glossary on pages 154 to 156.

Activities
These are the questions that you should complete after you have read the explanations and examples for each question type. After you have worked through all the questions, turn to pages 134 to 153 to check your answers. If you got any of the answers wrong, read the topic again, and then have another go at the questions. When you are sure that you understand a topic, tick the box beside it on the Contents page.

Tip
This text gives you helpful tips on how to tackle a particular question type.

Important
This text gives you useful information, rules and techniques you should remember.

Rough paper
This symbol shows that you will need to answer the question on rough paper.

At the end of the book, there is a timed Practice test. You should attempt this once you are sure that you understand all the question types.

Sentences, phrases and clauses

Sentences

A sentence is a group of words that expresses at least one complete thought or idea.

Sentences always contain at least one verb. Verbs are 'doing' or 'being' words. Verbs are often used to describe what the **subject** of a sentence is doing. You will learn more about verbs on pages 13 to 16.

'delivers' is the verb – the word that describes the action that is happening in the sentence.

The florist **delivers** the flowers.

'The florist' is the subject of this sentence and is doing the action.

The **object** of a sentence is the person or thing that the action is being done to. In the sentence above, 'the flowers' are the object. Some sentences might not have a subject or object, but they will always have a verb.

Come here! ← The verb in this sentence is 'Come', but there is no subject or object.

 This is how subjects and objects behave in all active sentences. In passive sentences, actions are done to subjects. See pages 17 and 18 for more information on active and passive sentences.

Phrases and clauses

Sentences are made up of **phrases** and **clauses**.

A phrase is a small group of words that go together as a unit of meaning. A phrase does not contain a verb, and so is not a complete sentence and does not make sense on its own.

the girl on the bicycle   in the garden   Ben and Fatima

A clause is a group of words that contains both a subject and a verb. There are two types of clauses: main (or independent) clauses and subordinate (or dependent) clauses.

A **main clause** is a complete sentence and makes sense on its own.

The baby smiled happily. ← This is complete. You do not need any other information to understand it.

A **subordinate clause** is incomplete and does not make sense on its own. Subordinate clauses often start with a **connective** – a joining word or phrase, such as **therefore**, **although** or **in addition**.

'When' is a connective here. You will learn more about connectives on pages 23 to 24.

When Claudia entered the room ← This is incomplete. You do not know what happened when she entered the room.

A subordinate clause adds extra information to the main clause. It can appear before, in the middle of or after the main clause. When it appears before the main clause, a comma is used to separate the two clauses.

When Claudia entered the room, the baby smiled happily.

When it appears after the main clause, there is no comma.

The baby smiled happily **when Claudia entered the room**.

Sentences, phrases and clauses

You may be asked to identify phrases, main clauses and subordinate clauses.

Identify whether these are phrases, main clauses or subordinate clauses.

1. long dark hair

2. she bought two shirts

3. if you wear sun cream

4. since it was raining

5. Amber was late for school

6. next to the chair

Start by looking for the examples that do not contain a verb. The groups of words 'long dark hair' and 'next to the chair' don't have any 'doing' or 'being' words in, so there are no verbs. This must mean that they are phrases.

Then look for the examples that do not make sense on their own. The groups of words 'if you wear sun cream' and 'since it was raining' don't make sense on their own. You can check that they do contain verbs – 'wear' and 'was' – so they are not phrases. They also have connectives, so these must be subordinate clauses.

The examples left – 'she bought two shirts' and 'Amber was late for school' – make sense on their own and contain both a verb – 'bought' and 'was' – and a subject – 'she' and 'Amber'. They must be main clauses.

Write your answers out clearly.

Answer: 1. **phrase**

2. **main clause**

3. **subordinate clause**

4. **subordinate clause**

5. **main clause**

6. **phrase**

Identify whether these are phrases, main clauses or subordinate clauses.

1. with great difficulty _____

2. although she was gravely ill _____

3. he felt very angry _____

4. a beautiful rainbow _____

5. the cat hissed menacingly _____

6. before I wash my hair _____

Schofield & Sims

Sentences, phrases and clauses

You can use your knowledge of phrases and clauses to identify different sentence types.

A **simple sentence** consists of one independent clause containing both a subject and a verb. A simple sentence can be a **statement**, a question, an exclamation or a command.

| Greyson baked a cake for dessert. | What are you doing? | How kind you are! | Get me some water! |

A **compound sentence** is made up of two independent clauses joined together with a connective. Each clause makes sense on its own.

The word 'but' is a connective. It joins the two independent clauses together.

Eleanor wants cereal, **but** Sanjay wants toast.

A **complex sentence** is made up of one independent clause and one or more dependent clauses. The dependent clause starts with a connective.

When it stops raining, we will go out to play.   You should brush your teeth **before you go to bed**.

These are dependent clauses. They do not make sense on their own.

You may be asked to identify simple sentences, compound sentences and complex sentences.

Identify whether this is a simple sentence, a compound sentence or a complex sentence.

As kangaroos have pouches to carry their young, they are marsupials.

The clause before the comma does not make sense on its own and starts with the connective 'as', so it is a dependent clause. The clause after the comma is an independent clause. This must be a complex sentence.

Answer: complex sentence

 Do not assume a sentence is a complex sentence just because it is long. For example, the sentence 'Hummingbirds are one of the smallest species of bird on the entire planet.' is long, but it is still a simple sentence because it consists of just one independent clause.

Identify whether these are simple sentences, compound sentences or complex sentences.

7.   My best friend lives in the house opposite me.   _____

8.   Although Umar was tired, he was too excited to go to sleep.   _____

9.   Ruth is very good at skateboarding and she is also a strong swimmer.   _____

10.   Along with the dragon, the giant panda is a national symbol of China.   _____

11.   The mayor gave a long, dull speech to the bored, impatient crowd.   _____

12.   My journey home from school typically takes twenty minutes,

      but today it took an hour.   _____

Paragraphs

Paragraphs are made up of one or more sentences that deal with a particular idea or theme.

Each new paragraph shows that a new idea or theme is being introduced. Paragraphs also make long sections of text easier to read by breaking it up into manageable chunks. A new paragraph is shown either by indenting the first line of the paragraph or by leaving a line between paragraphs. Either approach is fine, but you do not need to do both.

> Hadrian's Wall is a defensive wall that was built by the Romans during the rule of Hadrian, a Roman emperor. It is situated just south of the modern-day border between England and Scotland and is 73 miles long.
> Another famous wall, the Great Wall of China, was built across the historical northern borders of China. The earliest fortifications were built in the seventh century BCE.

A new paragraph introduces a new idea – in this case, a different wall in a different location.

Paragraphs are also used in **dialogue** to show when a different character begins speaking.

> Looking around anxiously, Ruya whispered, "Where are we?"
> Toby replied, "I have no idea." A frown moved across his face like a shadow.

The whole new sentence goes on the new line, not just the speech.

You may be asked to break up a passage into paragraphs.

Use the paragraph symbol **/** before each word that should start a new paragraph in this passage.

When travelling in France, it is always worth making time to visit the wonderful city of Nice. Located on the south-east coast by the Italian border, it is France's fifth largest city, and has been a favourite spot for tourists since the eighteenth century. Nice's climate is hot and sunny in summer and mild and dry in winter. The best time to visit is between May and September when the days will be long and warm. There is plenty to do in the city. The beautiful sunshine and clear air in Nice appealed to famous painters such as Marc Chagall and Henri Matisse, who were inspired to create some of their most notable works here. Some of these can be found in the local museums.

First, split the passage up into sections by identifying key themes. In this example, you could identify three different themes: the city, the climate and things to do. Then look for the start of each section, which gives you the start of the paragraph. Finally, put paragraph markers in at the right places.

Answer: ... eighteenth century. **/** Nice's climate ...   ... long and warm. **/** There is plenty to do ...

 Use the paragraph symbol **/** before each word that should start a new paragraph in this passage.

1. Poppy was excited about starting at her new school. She had just moved to a big city with her family and was hoping to make lots of new friends as soon as possible. On her first day, she sprang out of bed before her alarm clock went off and headed downstairs for breakfast. She poured the cereal so fast that half of it jumped back out of the bowl and clattered on to the floor. "Slow down!" said Mum. "School will wait." "I just don't want to be late," replied Poppy as she ran upstairs to get dressed.

Schofield & Sims

Nouns

A noun is the name given to a person, place, thing or concept. There are many different types of nouns, including **common nouns**, **proper nouns**, **collective nouns** and **abstract nouns**.

Common nouns are the general names given to things, places or people. They do not require a capital letter unless they begin a sentence. They can be singular or plural. Common nouns are often preceded by a **determiner** (see page 25) or by an adjective.

> My **teacher** gave me a special **card** for my **birthday**.
> The **king** told us that there are hundreds of **plants** growing in his **gardens**.

A **noun phrase** is a group of words that is based on a noun (or **pronoun**). This can include determiners, adjectives and relative clauses.

> The **boy** ◄──────────── Here, 'boy' is the noun and 'the' is the determiner.
> The tall **boy** in the red jumper ◄── This version also has the adjective 'tall' and the prepositional phrase 'in the red jumper'.
> The **one** who was sitting over there ◄── This noun phrase is based on the pronoun 'one' and uses a relative clause.

Proper nouns are specific or special names given to people, places or things. This could include titles, days of the week, months of the year or events. They always begin with a capital letter.

> Every **Christmas** my older sisters, **Nicole** and **Fleur**, come to visit us in **Manchester**.
> **King Henry VII** won the **Wars of the Roses**.

Collective nouns are the names given to a collection or group of things.

 TIP Noun phrases can be used to make a title. Count this as a single proper noun.

> A **pride** of lions lay basking in the sun.
> In the middle of the ocean, a **fleet** of ships gathered for a naval exercise.

Abstract nouns are the names given to feelings, concepts or ideas. They are things you can't see, hear, touch, smell or taste.

> **Trust** is an important quality when working in a group.
> I have a terrible **fear** of spiders.

 TIP Many abstract nouns end with the **suffixes** –ness, –ship, –hood, –nce or –tion. For example, **kindness**, **leadership**, **childhood**, **patience** and **motivation**.

Some nouns traditionally had masculine and feminine forms. It is useful to know how to form these, although many of the feminine forms are used less often now. Sometimes, there are completely different words for male and female nouns. However, some feminine nouns are made by adding the suffix –ess on to the end of the masculine noun.

Some nouns also have diminutive forms. A diminutive is a word formed by adding a group of letters to show that something is smaller than other things of the same type.

Masculine noun	Feminine noun
man	woman
boy	girl
hero	heroine
lion	lioness
god	goddess

Noun	Diminutive noun
duck	duckling
pig	piglet
book	booklet
kitchen	kitchenette
drop	droplet

Nouns

You need to be able to identify different types of noun.

Complete the table using words from the sentence below.

A flock of tourists had gathered together and were counting down to the start of New Year's Day.

First, identify any noun that contains a capital letter ('New Year's Day'). This must be a proper noun. Underline all three words because you need all three words for the name of the day.

Then look for a plural word ('tourists') and see if there is a noun before it ('flock'). This must be a collective noun.

This plural word ('tourists') must also be a noun. Since it's a general name for a type of person, it must be a common noun.

Finally, look for a word which describes a concept, idea or feeling that you can't see, hear, touch, taste or smell. You can use determiners to help identify the remaining noun if necessary. There are two determiners in this sentence – 'a' before 'flock' and 'the' before 'start'. You've already identified 'flock' as a collective noun. The other noun ('start') refers to something you can't sense. This must be an abstract noun.

Answer:

Common noun	**tourists**
Proper noun	**New Year's Day**
Collective noun	**flock**
Abstract noun	**start**

 Complete the table using words from the sentence below.

1. Fluffy is showing great affection towards her first litter of puppies.

Common noun	
Proper noun	
Collective noun	
Abstract noun	

 Some verbs and nouns are spelt the same, so you must pay close attention to the context. For example, the word 'love' is a verb in the sentence 'I **love** chocolate'. It is an abstract noun in the sentence 'Send my **love** to your family'.

2. With enthusiasm, Finley sprinted towards the pile of leaves and jumped in.

Common noun	
Proper noun	
Collective noun	
Abstract noun	

Schofield & Sims

Pronouns

Pronouns can be used instead of nouns to avoid repeating the same noun multiple times. They can be singular or plural. There are various types of pronoun. For more on how pronouns are used in writing, see page 101.

Personal pronouns are words that are used in place of a name when referring to a person. **I**, **you**, **me**, **he**, **she**, **it**, **him**, **her**, **we**, **they**, **us** and **them** are personal pronouns.

'They' replaces 'Marie and Curtis'.

Marie and Curtis stayed with Isla. **They** went to the cinema with **her**.

The pronoun 'her' replaces 'Isla'.

 The word 'its' does not contain an apostrophe when it is used as a possessive pronoun. It should not be mistaken for the **contraction** 'it's', which means 'it is' or 'it has'.

Possessive pronouns tell us who or what possesses something (who it belongs to). The words **mine**, **yours**, **his**, **hers**, **theirs** and **ours** are some possessive pronouns.

Abby and I both have new coats. **Mine** is more colourful than **hers**.

 Some possessive determiners (see page 25) can also be used as possessive pronouns if they replace a noun.

Relative pronouns add relative clauses into sentences. Relative clauses provide extra information about a subject or object. The words **who**, **whom**, **which** and **that** can all be used as relative pronouns.

The relative pronoun introduces a relative clause with additional information about the runner.

The runner, **who** had been about to win, tripped and fell.
The holiday **that** I've been planning my entire life was brilliant.

The relative pronoun specifies which holiday the sentence refers to.

Indefinite pronouns refer in general terms to people or things. For example, **something**, **everyone**, **anything**, **nobody** and **somewhere** are all indefinite pronouns.

You could replace 'No-one' with another noun or pronoun and the sentence would still make sense.

No-one wants to go fishing in the rain.

You should be able to replace nouns with pronouns in a sentence or short passage.

Rewrite the passage, replacing the repeated nouns with the appropriate pronouns.

Nicholas was very tired as Nicholas had been up all night with a stomach ache. Nicholas had called out for Nicholas's mother several times, but it had taken a few attempts before Nicholas's mother had heard Nicholas.

Look for the first repeated noun in the passage. This needs to stay the same to establish the identity of the subject. In this case, the noun is Nicholas. Then look for where the noun is repeated and replace it with the appropriate pronoun. Repeat this process for other repeated nouns in the passage (in this instance, 'Nicholas's mother').

Answer: Nicholas was very tired as **he** had been up all night with a stomach ache. **He** had called out for **his** mother several times, but it had taken a few attempts before **she** had heard **him**.

Rewrite the passage, replacing the repeated nouns with the appropriate pronouns.

1. During the summer, the Roberts family love to go on holiday to Dorset. The Roberts family always stay in the same hotel, which is called the Sunflower Hotel. The Sunflower Hotel is always busy, and Owen, the receptionist, is very friendly. Owen always greets all the guests with a smile and asks all the guests how all the guests are enjoying all the guests' stays.

Sometimes, you may be given a selection of pronouns to choose from and be asked to select the correct pronouns to complete a sentence.

> Underline the correct pronouns to complete the sentence.
>
> Simon was always happy to help *him / her / his* little sister with *she / his / her* homework.
>
> First, look at who is the subject of the sentence. Whether they are male, female or plural will tell you the correct pronoun to use. Simon is the subject of the sentence, and he is male, so the first pronoun is 'his'. Keep following this approach with the rest of the sentence. It looks like the homework belongs to Simon's sister, so the second pronoun is 'her'.
>
> **Answer:** Simon was always happy to help *him / her / <u>his</u>* little sister with *she / his / <u>her</u>* homework.

 Underline the correct pronouns to complete each sentence.

2. *Anything / Everything / Everyone* has gone wrong today, so I can't leave work just yet.

3. This is the friend *who / whom / which* lives two doors down from me.

4. You will know that it is *mine / theirs / our* house as it has a bright red door.

5. The dog had a beautiful diamond collar around *its / it's / him* neck.

6. *Anything / Anyone / Someone* who wants to join the club should sign up today.

7. Please give *your / hers / theirs* completed forms to *my / me / mine* as soon as possible.

8. My friends and *me / them / I* would love to go swimming tonight.

'I' or 'me'? 'Who' or 'whom'?

Use 'who' and 'I' when each is the **subject** of the sentence completing the action.

My sister and I love to eat Mexican food.

Who is coming tonight?

Use 'whom' and 'me' when each is the **object** of the sentence receiving the action.

My mum drove **my sister and me** to the arcade.

To **whom** did you speak?

Double check by taking out the extra person ('my sister') – if it still sounds right, you have it the right way around.

Verbs

A verb is a word that describes an action. It can also describe a state of being. The word 'is' is a verb and is often used to describe a state of being.

As you saw on page 5, sentences always contain at least one verb. The verb often tells you what is happening to the subject of the sentence.

 The basic form of a verb is called the infinitive. Infinitives **do not** have a subject and are not the main verb in a sentence. You can usually identify infinitives because they have 'to' in front of them. For example, **to smile**, **to be**, **to remember**.

Olivia **paints** a portrait. ⟵⟶ 'Olivia' is the subject and 'paints' describes an action.
The cat **is** full. ⟵⟶ 'The cat' is the subject and 'is' describes a state of being.

The verb and subject of a sentence must agree in number and person. A singular subject needs a singular verb, and a plural subject needs a plural verb.

I **am** excited. ⟵⟶ Subject and verb are singular and first person.
Blake **is** excited. ⟵⟶ Subject and verb are singular and third person.
Miraj and Lola **are** excited. ⟵ Subject and verb are plural and third person.

You need to be able to identify the verb in a sentence.

> Underline the main verb or verbs in the sentence.
>
> How many children cycle to school every day?

Start by identifying the subject of the sentence (who or what is 'being' or 'doing' something if the sentence is active). Then look for the being or doing word (the verb) connected to the subject.

The subject is 'children'. The verb connected to the subject is 'cycle'. When you have found your verb, underline it carefully.

Answer: How many children <u>cycle</u> to school every day?

 Underline the main verb or verbs in each sentence.

1. I adore my mother's deliciously sweet chocolate cake.

2. In the mornings, the birds up in the trees sing so loudly.

3. Sometimes I catch the bus to school with my friends despite the very long queue at the bus stop.

4. She was very tired yesterday due to an extremely long and busy day at the office.

5. In winter, heavy snowfall often causes severe delays to train services.

6. Today, I went to the park with my whole family and we had a picnic.

Verbs

Verbs can describe actions that happen in the past, the present or the future. The tense of the verb tells you when something is happening.

Simple tenses

The simple tenses describe things that happen once and then stop ('They bake cookies together'), or things that happen regularly ('He bakes bread every Saturday').

In the past and the present, the form of the verb changes depending on the subject. For regular verbs, you often need to add –s with 'he', 'she' or 'it', and –ed in the past. You use 'will' to show that an action is happening in the future.

Past
I bak**ed**

Present
She bake**s**

Future
You **will** bake

 TIP In English, you add the verb 'will' to the present form of the verb to express the future. Any extra verbs that you add on like this are called **auxiliary verbs**. You also use auxiliary verbs to make the progressive tenses and the perfect tenses.

Progressive tenses

The progressive tenses describe actions that keep going over a period of time ('They are baking a cake'). The main verb is used in its –ing form.

Then you add the right form of the verb 'to be' in front to show whether the action is happening in the past, present or future.

Past progressive
I **was** bak**ing**

Present progressive
She **is** bak**ing**

Future progressive
You **will be** bak**ing**

 The progressive tenses are also sometimes described as the continuous tenses.

Perfect tenses

You often use the perfect tenses before another tense to show what order events happened in ('After we had baked cookies, we ate them') or to show consequences ('She has baked bread, so she does not need to buy any').

To make a perfect tense, you take the past form of the main verb and add the right form of the verb 'to have' in front to show whether the action is happening in the past, present or future.

Past perfect
I **had baked**

Present perfect
She **has baked**

Future perfect
You **will have baked**

 Some verbs do not follow the usual patterns. Those that do not are called irregular verbs. For instance, you say 'I thought' not 'I thinked'. You must learn the forms of irregular verbs. A list of the most common irregular verbs can be found on the Schofield & Sims website.

Verbs

You must be able to identify the tense of a verb in a sentence.

> Identify whether the verb in this sentence is in the past tense, the present tense or the future tense.
>
> The team will play an important football game on Sunday.

First, look at who or what is doing the action and when it is happening.

In this sentence, 'the team' will be doing the action. They will be playing a football game. The auxiliary verb 'will' in 'will play' is a clue that the verb is in the future tense.

Answer: future tense

Sometimes, you might need to think carefully to identify the main verb in the sentence.

> Identify whether the verb in this sentence is in the past tense, the present tense or the future tense.
>
> Sophia enjoys swimming in the sea.

In this sentence, it may look like there is more than one verb: 'enjoys' and 'swimming'. Always choose the verb which is directly connected to the subject. Here, 'Sophia' is the subject, so the verb connected to her is 'enjoys'. This verb is in the present tense.

Answer: present tense

 Remember that some verbs are irregular.

 Identify whether the verb in each sentence is in the past tense, the present tense or the future tense.

7. I will be wearing my favourite green and yellow hat to the wedding

    ceremony on Saturday.   _____

8. During the party, an enormous birthday cake was presented to Samir.   _____

9. As a hobby, I build model train sets for my younger sister.   _____

10. My grandfather is teaching me to play chess at the weekends.   _____

11. I will buy a special present for my teacher as a thank you for all her

    hard work over the year.   _____

12. Every morning, we see long traffic jams as we cycle to school.   _____

Verbs

Sometimes, you may be asked to rewrite a sentence using the correct tense of the verb. If there are several verbs in the sentence, you must make sure that they make sense together.

One verb has been used incorrectly in the sentence. Underline the incorrect verb and write the correct form of the verb on the line.

Right now, my friend is cooked a delicious curry for everyone in

the kitchen.

_____

First, you need to work out when the action is taking place. The sentence begins with the phrase 'right now' so you can tell that the action is happening in the present and is ongoing.

Then you need to identify the verb. **Scan** the sentence to identify the subject and verb. You can see that 'my friend' is the subject, 'cooked' is the main verb and 'is' is an auxiliary verb. Both 'is' and 'cooked' agree with the subject, but they do not make sense together.

 Sometimes, words you would normally think of as verbs may be acting as another word class in a sentence. For example, the word 'play' can be a verb, like in the sentence 'We **play** outside for an hour every day after school'. It can also be a noun, like in the sentence 'I saw a **play** yesterday'.

Since the action is in the present and is ongoing, you will need to make them into the present continuous tense. The word 'is' can stay the same, but 'cooked' needs to change to 'cooking'.

Check that your new sentence makes sense by reading it back with the new verb in place. It does, so this is the answer.

Answer: Right now, my friend is <u>cooked</u> a delicious curry for everyone in the kitchen.   **cooking**

 One verb has been used incorrectly in each sentence. Underline the incorrect verb and write the correct form of the verb on the line.

13. Last Christmas, I giving my friend a special present that I had

made myself.

_____

14. "Quick! Someone is came!" she shouted.

_____

15. I will got lost if I do not take a map.

_____

16. The postal worker delivers a very strange parcel yesterday.

_____

17. "Where were you? I sit on my own for ages," he complained.

_____

18. "Made sure you tidy up after you have finished cooking,"

demanded Shirley.

_____

Active and passive sentences

A sentence is written in an **active voice** when the subject of the sentence performs the action.

Jessica **writes** a letter.

In this sentence, Jessica, the subject, is performing the action of writing.

A sentence is written in the **passive voice** when the subject of the sentence has an action done to it by someone or something else.

A letter **was written** by Jessica.

Here, the subject of the sentence is the letter. Although it is not doing the action (writing), it still comes before the verb and must match the verb in number and person.

In both these sentences the subject comes first. However, in the active sentence the subject is performing the action, and in the passive sentence the subject is having the action performed on it.

You may be asked to identify whether a sentence is active or passive.

Identify whether the sentence is active or passive.

Harry was hit by the ball after it was kicked energetically by Rana.

First, identify the subjects and the verbs. In this sentence there are several. The subjects are 'Harry' and 'it', meaning 'the ball'. The verbs are 'was hit' and 'was kicked'. Both of these verbs begin with forms of 'to be' and are showing that an action is being done to one of the subjects. Both parts of this complex sentence are passive. This is a passive sentence.

Answer: passive

Identify whether each sentence is active or passive.

1. I hope that the man and woman will stop talking when the film starts. _____

2. The residents are very angry at the planned changes to

   parking regulations. _____

3. This year, our team's colours were changed from blue and

   orange to purple and green. _____

4. The hockey match should have been postponed when rain

   was forecast. _____

5. On Saturday, it was very windy, and Verity's hat blew away. _____

6. All the new games consoles were bought by enthusiastic customers

   before the release date. _____

(!) Passive sentences can use any form of 'to be' with another verb.

Active and passive sentences

You may be asked to change an active sentence into a passive sentence or vice versa.

Rewrite the active sentences in the passive voice and the passive sentences in the active voice.

Amy greedily ate a double scoop ice cream in record time.

In this sentence the subject, Amy, is performing the action, so it must be an active sentence. Swap the subjects around so that the ice cream is written about at the beginning of the sentence. As it will be receiving the action, the verb form 'ate' must change to the passive 'was eaten'.

Answer: A double scoop ice cream was eaten greedily by Amy in record time.

 TIP Try lightly underlining the subject, verb and object before you try to rearrange the sentence. You'll then be able to see what needs to move. Remember to move the whole noun phrase (see page 9), not just the noun.

Rewrite the active sentences in the passive voice and the passive sentences in the active voice.

An old letter from a member of the royal household dating back hundreds of years was discovered by a resident of Blenheim Road in Cornwall.

Here, you reverse the process. The sentence is currently passive because the subject (the letter) is having the action performed on it. Swap the subjects around, so that the resident is written about at the beginning of the sentence, and change the verb form to the active form 'discovered an old letter'.

Answer: A resident of Blenheim Road in Cornwall discovered an old letter from a member of the royal household dating back hundreds of years.

 Rewrite the active sentences in the passive voice and the passive sentences in the active voice.

7. A speeding train crashed into a deserted station when its brakes failed.

_____

8. I was given a very generous present by my auntie last week.

_____

9. A massive snowball was hurled at my little sister by my brother.

_____

10. After dinner, he ate a whole plate of biscuits.

_____

 Make sure you include the correct subject/verb agreement with 'to be' when writing in the passive voice:

I was   you were   he/she/it was   we were   they were

Schofield & Sims

Prepositions

Prepositions show the position of something (a noun or pronoun) in relation to something else.

This can be in relation to location, direction or time.

The dog hid **under** the pile of newspapers. ← location
The dog sped **across** the road. ← direction
The dog escaped **after** sunset. ← time

 TIP The word 'position' in 'pre**position**' is a useful reminder of what they do: they identify the position of things.

You may be asked to find the preposition in a sentence or short passage.

Underline the preposition in the sentence. Then identify whether it shows a location, direction or time relationship.

The storm continued throughout the night.

First, look for two nouns or pronouns within each sentence. In this case, you will find the words 'storm' and 'night'.

Then identify the word which connects the nouns or pronouns in terms of location, direction or time. These are the prepositions. There can be more than one preposition in a sentence. In this case, 'throughout' connects the nouns through time.

Answer: The storm continued <u>throughout</u> the night.   **time**

 TIP If you need to narrow it down further, you can ignore any words that you know are from another word class. For example, 'continued' here is a verb, so it cannot be a preposition; 'the' is a determiner, so it cannot be a preposition. This leaves you with 'throughout'.

 Underline the preposition in each sentence. Then identify whether each one shows a location, direction or time relationship.

1. The papers were scattered around the room.

_____

2. Everyone ran towards the bus stop.

_____

3. The restaurant didn't open until noon.

_____

4. She hasn't completed any homework since Wednesday.

_____

5. He knew there was a special gift inside the box.

_____

6. At school, we had a wonderful surprise assembly.

_____

> **!** To remember prepositions relating to time, imagine events on a timeline and identify the order in which they occur.
> I had breakfast → I went to school
> **before**

Prepositions

Sometimes, you may be given a selection of prepositions to choose from to complete a sentence.

Choose the correct prepositions from the box below to complete each sentence. Use each preposition once.

from	down	at	above	into
through	until	to	between	atop

Tears of joy ran _____ her cheeks as she realised she had won first prize.

First, look at the rest of the sentence to work out whether the preposition needs to be related to location, direction or time. In this case, it should be direction, so cross out any others. This leaves you with 'from', 'down', 'into', 'through', 'to' and 'between'. Then choose an appropriate preposition that makes sense in this context. 'Down' makes the most sense, so this is the answer.

Answer: Tears of joy ran **down** her cheeks as she realised she had won first prize.

TIP If you think more than one word could fit in the gap and you have several sentences to fill, move on to the next sentence. Go back to any sentences you have left at the end to see what options you still have: you may have used some of the options in different sentences.

 Choose the correct prepositions from the box below to complete each sentence. Use each preposition once.

7.

next to	up	inside	on	before
with	at	during	over	in

i) The horse jumped _____ the fence.

ii) You must finish writing your letter _____ you eat your snack.

iii) _____ playtime, she had to practise playing the piano.

iv) It took all day for me to climb _____ the mountain.

v) Hang the dress _____ the wardrobe _____ the orange skirt.

vi) I will help you _____ a moment.

vii) I am going to the park _____ my sister.

viii) I must visit my uncle _____ exactly 10.00 a.m. _____ Thursday.

Adjectives

Adjectives are words that describe nouns or pronouns.

Positive adjectives add extra detail by clarifying or modifying these words in a number of ways. For example, they can describe colours and patterns (**crimson** tie, **striped** shirt, **spotted** handkerchief), size (**colossal** statue, **gargantuan** appetite, **minuscule** insect) and emotions (**joyful** celebration, **anxious** job applicant, **angry** dog).

To compare two things or people, you use a **comparative adjective**. Comparative adjectives often contain the suffix –er, or –ier if the adjective ends in –y. If the adjective contains more than one syllable, often the word 'more' or 'less' is added to the adjective instead. After each comparative, add the word 'than'.

The oak tree is **wider than** the sycamore tree in the other garden.
I have baked biscuits that are far **more delicious than** yours!

Superlative adjectives are used to compare three or more things. The word 'the' precedes the superlative. Often, the suffix –est or –iest is added, or the phrase 'the most' or 'the least'.

Ben Nevis is **the highest** mountain in the British Isles.
Cheese and onion is **the least popular** flavour of crisps in our class.

You may be asked to identify whether a word is a positive adjective, a comparative adjective or a superlative adjective.

Identify whether the word is a positive adjective, a comparative adjective or a superlative adjective.

farthest

First, see whether you recognise the adjective or its root. This word looks like it might come from the word 'far', which is a positive adjective. However, it does look irregular because of the extra 'th'. Since the word here is 'farthest' not 'far', you know that this is a comparative or a superlative.

Then look at its suffix. If it had an –er suffix, it would be comparative. Since it has the suffix –est, it is likely to be superlative. The sequence 'far', 'farther', 'farthest' makes sense, so this is a superlative adjective.

Answer: superlative adjective

 Identify whether these words are positive adjectives, comparative adjectives or superlative adjectives.

1. most brave   _____

2. kind   _____

3. youngest   _____

4. filthier   _____

5. easier   _____

6. cloudy   _____

7. most famous   _____

8. less powerful   _____

Adverbs

An **adverb** is a word that describes or gives more information about a verb. Adverbs describe how, when, where, how often and to what extent something happens.

I visit the dentist **regularly** to maintain healthy teeth. We must ensure that the concert starts **punctually**.

We will have to stay **inside** as it is raining. She finished the exam **quickly**.

Adverbs can also describe or give more information about adjectives or other adverbs.

The adverb 'extremely' modifies the adjective 'important'.

It is **extremely** important that you finish all your homework. Thea practised her dance routine **very carefully**.

Here there are two adverbs. The word 'very' modifies the adverb 'carefully', which describes the verb.

(!) Many adverbs of the 'how' type end with the suffix –ly. For example, **quickly**, **diligently**, **ferociously**.

You may be asked to identify the adverbs in a sentence or passage.

> Underline the adverbs in the passage.
>
> It was midnight. Dark clouds rolled ominously across the inky-black sky. Low rumbles of thunder could be heard gradually building in volume and bright flashes of lightning completely lit up the horizon. I had begun the night feeling quite anxious, but I was now very scared!

First, identify the verbs which have extra information attached to them. In this case, 'rolled', 'building' and 'lit' all have extra information either before or after them – 'ominously', 'gradually' and 'completely'. These are all adverbs. Notice that they all end in –ly.

Next, look for adjectives which have extra information attached to them. In this case 'anxious' has the adverb 'quite' before it and 'scared' has the adverb 'very' before it.

'Now' is also telling us when this is happening, so it is an adverb. Underline all these words.

Answer:

It was midnight. Dark clouds rolled <u>ominously</u> across the inky-black sky. Low rumbles of thunder could be heard <u>gradually</u> building in volume and bright flashes of lightning <u>completely</u> lit up the horizon. I had begun the night feeling <u>quite</u> anxious, but I was <u>now</u> <u>very</u> scared!

 Underline the adverbs in the passage.

1. The bell rang sonorously – it would soon be time to go home from school. I was really terribly excited as it was my birthday and I was anticipating a warm welcome from my family when I got home. Eventually, after a long wait for my friend to catch up with me, we raced merrily down the street. I was thinking about the delicious chocolate birthday cake that I had baked with Dad yesterday. I couldn't wait to gobble it up greedily when I got home.

22

Connectives

A connective is a word or phrase that joins one word, clause or sentence to another. Connectives can be **conjunctions**, prepositions or adverbs. Two of the most important types of conjunction are **co-ordinating conjunctions** and **subordinating conjunctions**.

Co-ordinating conjunctions

Co-ordinating conjunctions can join two main clauses together in a compound sentence. This makes both parts of the sentence seem equally important.

These two pieces of information are separate and make sense on their own. They can be linked with the co-ordinating conjunction 'and'.

On Saturday, I went to the cinema with my friends **and** we watched a new action film.

> **TIP** Co-ordinating conjunctions:
> **FOR AND NOR BUT OR YET SO**
>
> You can use the mnemonic **FANBOYS** to remember them.

We will have to eat at home tonight, **for** the restaurant is completely booked.

Like 'because', the co-ordinating conjunction 'for' is used to give a reason.

Subordinating conjunctions

Subordinating conjunctions can join a main clause and a subordinate clause together to make a complex sentence. Subordinating conjunctions let you add extra information to a sentence, such as an explanation.

The subordinating conjunction 'because' introduces an explanation.

They didn't play tennis **because** it was raining.

> **TIP** There are lots of subordinating conjunctions. Some common ones are: **if**, **while**, **although**, **whereas**, **because**, **since**, **as**, **unless**, **until** and **despite**.

Martina will look for her keys **until** she finds them.

The subordinating conjunction 'until' adds additional information about when Martina will stop looking for her keys.

You can use subordinating conjunctions at the start of a sentence if the subordinate clause comes before the main clause. When the subordinate clause comes first, put a comma between it and the main clause.

The subordinate clause could go after the main clause and the sentence would still make sense.

Although the sea was cold**,** Evan decided to go swimming.

Remember to add the comma between the two clauses.

If you want to get to the town centre**,** take the bus from the train station.

The subordinating conjunction 'if' is used to write about something that might happen.

Other connectives

Other phrases can be used to link sentences together in a paragraph. Connectives can help you link ideas together and create cohesion in your writing because they show how different parts of the text fit together. Common connectives include words and phrases like **even though**, **however**, **in addition**, **therefore**, **consequently** and **due to**.

This connective links the information in the first sentence to the information in the second sentence.

I ran around a lot at lunchtime. **As a result,** I was quite tired by the end of the day.

On the one hand, Caitlyn loved the idea of a holiday in Spain. **On the other hand,** she hated flying.

'One the one hand, ... On the other hand, ...' shows a contrast between two ideas in two sentences.

Connectives

You may be asked to identify connectives in a passage.

> Underline the connectives in the passage.
>
> The Sahara Desert covers most of northern Africa, yet it is still only the third largest desert in the world. However, it is the hottest, reaching temperatures over 40°C. Although very dry today, some experts predict it will become lush and green in around 15 000 years.
>
> **Answer:**
>
> The Sahara Desert covers most of northern Africa, <u>yet</u> it is still only the third largest desert in the world. <u>However</u>, it is the hottest, reaching temperatures over 40°C. <u>Although</u> very dry today, some experts predict it will become lush and green in around 15 000 years.

 Underline the connectives in the passage.

1. My grandfather died before I was born. Since he was a gentle man, he had enjoyed working as a nurse in a children's ward. I was told that he was also a proficient musician and could play several musical instruments.

Some questions may ask you to choose the most appropriate connective to complete a sentence.

> Underline the connective that would complete the sentence in the best way.
>
> My favourite lesson in school is science *if / but / because* I love doing experiments.
>
> Try to work out the meaning of the sentence by looking at how the two clauses relate to each other. Then choose the connective that fits that meaning. If you are unsure, you could also try out each connective in the sentence and see which makes the most sense. The word 'because' makes the most sensible link between the clauses. It is the most appropriate connective to use.
>
> **Answer:** My favourite lesson in school is science *if / but / <u>because</u>* I love doing experiments.

 Underline the connective that would complete each sentence in the best way.

2. *While / During / Since* I was doing my homework, a huge spider crawled across my desk.

3. Sienna was picked for the netball team *if / despite / because* only just returning from injury.

4. Deepak wanted cheese sandwiches for lunch *because / so / whereas* Darren wanted chicken salad.

5. She practised for many hours for her piano exam. *Nevertheless / As a result / On the other hand,* she passed with a mark of distinction.

Determiners

A determiner is a word that is placed in front of a noun or a noun phrase to make it clear which person or thing you are referring to, and whether you mean just one or more than one.

There are several different types of determiner:

Definite articles – **the** stray dog, **the** book on **the** table

Indefinite articles – **an** apple, **a** beautiful picture

Possessive determiners (showing what belongs to whom) – **my**, **your**, **her**, **his**, **their**, **our**, **its**

Interrogative determiners (often go before a question) – **what**, **which**, **whose**

Quantifiers (how many) – **some**, **many**, **few**, **more**, **less**, **several**, **any**, **a lot of**, **enough**, **all**, **one**, **two**

 TIP Remember that if the next word after the determiner begins with a vowel sound, you use 'an' instead of 'a': **a b**ruised banana; **an a**mazing adventure.

When the word begins with 'h', use 'a' or 'an' depending on whether you pronounce the 'h' sound or not: **a h**orse; **an h**our.

You may be asked to identify the determiner in a sentence or passage.

> Underline the determiners in the passage.
>
> It was a warm, sunny day. The sky was blue, and several birds could be seen building their nests in preparation for the arrival of new-born chicks.

First, identify the nouns in the passage. In this case, they are 'day', 'sky', 'birds', 'nests', 'arrival' and 'chicks'.

Then look for the determiner that comes before each of these nouns:

day – **a** (indefinite article)

sky – **the** (definite article)

birds – **several** (quantifier)

nests – **their** (possessive determiner)

arrival – **the** (definite article)

chicks – no apparent determiner

Answer:

It was <u>a</u> warm, sunny day. <u>The</u> sky was blue, and <u>several</u> birds could be seen building <u>their</u> nests in preparation for <u>the</u> arrival of new-born chicks.

 Underline the determiners in each sentence.

1. His room was large and spacious with many bookcases and enough books

    squeezed on to them to fill a library!

2. I gave every orange-flavoured sweet I found to my sister.

3. Do you know if we have any pencils left in the stationery cupboard?

4. Those flowers are so beautiful and look perfect in that vase.

5. Which dessert would you like to choose from this delicious selection?

6. An angry customer charged through the shop like a raging rhinoceros.

Grammar practice page 1

Now test your skills with these practice pages. If you get stuck, go back to pages 5 to 25 for some reminders.

Sentences, phrases and clauses

Identify whether these are phrases, main clauses or subordinate clauses.

1. several days later   _____

2. however bad it may seem   _____

3. under the stars   _____

4. I wish it were Saturday   _____

5. since it was raining   _____

6. sharks hunt for food   _____

Identify whether these are simple sentences, compound sentences or complex sentences.

7. The sun finally came out later that day.   _____

8. We have to go to bed when the clock strikes 10.   _____

9. The black and white dog ran after the red and blue ball. _____

10. Since it is raining, you had better take your umbrella. _____

11. In order for me to win the race, I must train hard every day. _____

12. I love going to the cinema, but I also enjoy live theatre. _____

Paragraphs

Use the paragraph symbol **/** before each word that should start a new paragraph in this passage.

13. It was the first day of term at Aleena's new school. She was thrilled to be starting Year 7 at Suchford Grammar. At the bus stop, Aleena's friend Alex was already waiting for her. The bus arrived promptly, and they rushed to the back to chat with their other friends, who were already on the bus. "I can't wait to see who my new teacher is," declared Aleena, and they all agreed that they were just so nervous and excited all at the same time. As the bus approached the school, they could see a huge sign saying, 'Welcome Year 7'. Today was going to be a fantastic day!

Nouns

14. Complete the table using words from the sentence below.

Yesterday, Amaal gave me a beautiful bouquet of crimson and lavender flowers for my birthday.

Common noun	
Proper noun	
Collective noun	
Abstract noun	

Schofield & Sims

Pronouns

 Rewrite the passage, replacing the repeated nouns with the appropriate pronouns.

1. Jamil needed to buy some new shoes. Jamil had just passed Jamil's music exam, so Jamil's mother let Jamil pick the music in Jamil's mother's car on the drive to the shop. Jamil tried on a pair of trainers in Jamil's favourite colour. Jamil exclaimed, "These feel great! They fit Jamil perfectly!"

Underline the correct pronouns to complete each sentence.

2. It was nice of *him / anybody / them* to bring *its / his / she* dog along to the park.

3. People *who / that / which* exercise regularly are normally quite fit.

Verbs

Underline the main verb or verbs in each sentence.

4. No matter how hard I try, I can't hit the highest note of the song.

5. After a long day at school, I jump straight into a hot, bubbly bath.

6. Ever since I was young, I have loved watching game shows.

Identify whether the verb in each sentence is in the past tense, the present tense or the future tense.

7. It is a long and arduous journey to the holiday resort. _____

8. You will need to act responsibly on the school trip. _____

9. Helen ate her soup very slowly and carefully. _____

One verb has been used incorrectly in each sentence. Underline the incorrect verb and write the correct form of the verb on the line.

10. Yesterday, I went fishing and catch a huge fish that I took home

    and will cook for dinner tonight. _____

11. Normally, I like to watch my favourite TV programme in my bedroom,

    but today my family sitting in the lounge and enjoyed it together. _____

12. Next year, my sister wants to went to the sixth-form college

    near our house. _____

13. Every Wednesday, I played hockey with my team

    and afterwards we all eat pizza together. _____

Active and passive sentences

Identify whether each sentence is active or passive.

1. The milk had been knocked over by a mischievous cat. _____

2. Mina painted the wall a vibrant shade of green. _____

3. The actors performed a modern version of Shakespeare's *Macbeth*. _____

Rewrite the active sentence in the passive voice and the passive sentence in the active voice.

4. The talent competition was won by the young amateur magician.

   _____

5. Sheila baked a delicious apple pie yesterday.

   _____

Prepositions

Underline the preposition in each sentence. Then identify whether each one shows a location, direction or time relationship.

6. During winter, it is important to wrap up warm. _____

7. The world beneath the surface of the sea is truly fascinating. _____

8. A solitary seagull soared through the clouds. _____

9. I will go to netball club after school. _____

Choose the correct prepositions from the box below to complete each sentence. Use each preposition once.

10.

after	up	through	on
against	between	until	past

i) Megan and Logan shared the sweets _____ them.

ii) He leant _____ the wall while he waited for his friend.

iii) The hungry dog ran straight _____ his food, unaware of his mistake.

iv) _____ dinner, we can watch your favourite programme if you like.

v) All _____ the night he sat and listened to the sound of owls hooting.

vi) Please wait _____ everyone has finished before you leave the table.

vii) They climbed _____ the stairs and waited _____ the platform for the train.

Adjectives

Identify whether these words are positive adjectives, comparative adjectives or superlative adjectives.

1. the longest _____

2. infrequent _____

3. easier _____

4. less fortunate _____

5. oblivious _____

6. the most fascinating _____

Adverbs

Underline the adverbs in the passage.

7. Children frequently flock to the shop where Leona regularly sells misshapen sweets and broken

chocolate bars for half price. The sweets are very popular. Their brightly coloured wrappers

enchant the children, and they can't wait to get their hands on the eagerly awaited prize.

Connectives

Underline the connectives in the passage.

8. I tried very hard to win the obstacle course, but I was unsuccessful. After I had managed to jump

over the hurdles, I slipped while I was weaving through the cones. I ended up finishing behind

everyone else. However, I didn't mind because I won the egg and spoon race!

Underline the connective that would complete each sentence in the best way.

9. *Despite / Since / As* the cold weather, we decided to go for a long walk in the woods.

10. The cat meows enthusiastically *wherever / whenever / as ever* her owner returns.

11. I would love to be a vet when I grow up *as / so / although* I've always enjoyed helping animals.

12. The grass has grown very long, *since / so / because* I will have to mow the lawn later.

Determiners

Underline the determiners in each sentence.

13. These snacks look delicious – I am going to take two biscuits.

14. Whose socks are lying all over the floor?

15. Do you know where the folder is that I left on the table?

16. Do you have enough money for that fairground ride?

17. My cousin gave me an elegant green dress for Christmas.

Sentence punctuation

Punctuation marks show the reader where sentences start and finish. They also make writing easier to understand and help you to communicate your message effectively.

Look at this sentence:

> david enjoys cooking his family and his dog

Without punctuation, it sounds as if David is a cannibal!

> **D**avid enjoys cooking**,** his family and his dog**.**

With the correct punctuation, it's clear that David doesn't want to cook his family or his dog after all!

There are some basic punctuation marks you should be confident using.

Capital letters

Capital letters must be used at the beginning of every sentence.

> **H**e stopped and stared. **S**omething was creeping across the floor making strange noises.

Capital letters are also always used for:

- specific names of people and places

Jeremy	**P**aris
Sarah **J**enkins	**T**ennyson **S**treet
Mr **K**umar	**M**ount **E**tna

 TIP These words need capitals because they are proper nouns. For more information on proper nouns, see page 9.

- specific names of days, months (but not seasons), special events and festivals

Monday	**E**id
February	**Y**om **K**ippur
Christmas	**N**ew **Y**ear's **E**ve

- specific names of organisations and brands, and acronyms or initialisms

United **N**ations	**MOT**
RSPCA	**ASAP**

- titles of artistic works, such as books, films, plays and music.

Black Beauty	*Romeo and Juliet*
Peter Pan	*The Nutcracker Suite*

 If a title has lots of little words in it, such as 'and' or 'the', they are written with lower case letters unless they begin or end the title.

Sentence punctuation

Several different punctuation marks can be used to end a sentence.

Full stops

Full stops are used at the end of statements. A statement is a sentence that gives information or an opinion.

This statement is a fact.

It is 10 o'clock. I think you should go to bed. ◄— This statement provides an opinion.

Question marks

Question marks are used when asking a direct question. Look out for question words, such as **what**, **how**, **why**, **when**, **where** and **who**. Groups of words like **is this** or **do you** can also indicate questions.

What would happen if we added baking powder to the cake mixture?
Do you want to come with me to the shops?

 You do not need to use a question mark when you are reporting a question rather than asking one directly.

Exclamation marks

Exclamation marks are used to show a dramatic emotion such as surprise, shock, anger, amazement or disgust. Often a character might be shouting when an exclamation mark is used – you should be able to tell this from the context.

Exclamation marks can also be used with commands and with exclamations.

| Stop right there! | Slow down! ◄——————— These are commands – they use command verbs. |
| How nice you look! | What a long day that was! ◄—— These are exclamations – they use 'how' or 'what'. |

Ellipses

Ellipses are three dots used to leave out words or phrases. They also show where a thought is unfinished or has been interrupted.

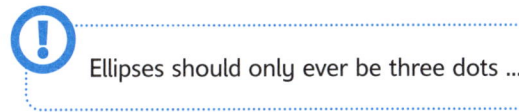 Ellipses should only ever be three dots ...

This ellipsis shows that Bailey's first thought was never finished. After reading it, you know that he won't finish that thought in the next sentence.

"Perhaps you can borrow my book ..." began Bailey. "No, wait. I need it for my homework tonight."

Ellipses are also used to create a dramatic effect such as a cliffhanger to keep the reader in suspense.

This ellipsis also marks missing information – you don't know **why** it is too late. This makes you want to keep reading.

As he walked deeper and deeper into the forest, he knew he should turn back. But it was too late ...

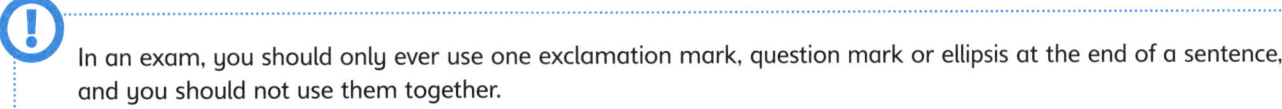 In an exam, you should only ever use one exclamation mark, question mark or ellipsis at the end of a sentence, and you should not use them together.

You may be asked to spot punctuation mistakes in a sentence or passage. You may also be asked to pick the sentence that is punctuated correctly out of a set of sentences or you might have to decide whether there is a mistake or not in a section of a sentence.

> Circle the punctuation mistakes in this passage.
>
> it was a cold and dark night. before he knew it, jake found himself alone in the park. where were his family He had to find out. Suddenly, a bright. flash shot down from the sky, a spaceship appeared and some aliens came out. What strange creatures they were

Work through the passage slowly looking for mistakes that definitely need to be fixed. The word 'it' starts the first sentence, so needs a capital 'I'. There is a full stop after 'night', so a capital letter is needed immediately after it. The proper noun 'jake' needs a capital 'J'. 'where' is after a full stop, so it needs a capital letter. It is also a question word introducing a direct question, so a question mark is needed after 'family'. 'Suddenly, a bright.' is not a complete sentence, so the full stop is not needed here. The final sentence is an exclamation starting with the word 'What'. An exclamation mark is needed here. Circle all these mistakes.

Answer: ⟨i⟩t was a cold and dark night. ⟨b⟩efore he knew it,⟨ ⟩⟨j⟩ake found himself alone in the park. ⟨w⟩here were his family⟨ ⟩He had to find out. Suddenly, a bright⟨.⟩ flash shot down from the sky, a spaceship appeared and some aliens came out. What strange creatures they were⟨ ⟩

Which sentence is punctuated correctly?

A. The River Thames runs through the capital city of England.

B. The river Thames runs through the capital city of England.

C. The River Thames runs through the Capital City of England.

D. The river thames runs through the capital City of England.

This sentence contains two proper nouns, so start by identifying them. 'England' and 'River Thames' are both names of things, so they need capital letters – in this case 'river' is part of a name. Therefore, B and D cannot be the correct answer and you can discount them.

Now look at the remaining options. The difference between A and C is that 'capital city' is capitalised. The phrase 'capital city' is not a name – the proper noun for this city is 'London' – so it does not need to be capitalised. Therefore, A must be the correct answer.

Answer: A

 Circle the punctuation mistakes in this passage.

1. at the beach in brighton, hundreds of families were enjoying their summer holidays children were splashing in the sea, and robert and. Jane were snorkelling. What more could anyone wish for Suddenly, there was a scream. "Help Help I've lost my watch" cried a child Luckily, someone dived down to the seabed to retrieve it.

Circle the letter of the sentence that is punctuated correctly.

2. **A.** Suddenly, the lights went down ... the film was about to start?

B. Suddenly, the lights went down ... the film was about to start.

C. Suddenly, the lights ... went down the film was about to start!

D. Suddenly, the lights went down? The film was about to start ...

Commas

Commas have many different functions. These are some of the most important ones.

1. They separate items (single words or short phrases) in a list to make the list easier to read.

I must remember my pen, pencil, ruler and eraser for the exam.
I enjoy riding my bicycle, playing with my friends, going to the cinema and learning to cook.
Would you like vanilla, chocolate or strawberry ice cream?

 The last two items in a list should be separated by the word 'and' (or sometimes 'or') instead of a comma. Occasionally you find **idioms** that use a comma instead, but this is rare.

2. They separate adjectives that are interchangeable.

The cold, gloomy cellar ⟵ These adjectives could be swapped around, so they need a comma between them.

3. They can be used to separate subordinate clauses from main clauses when the subordinate clause comes at the start of the sentence. They can also be used around **embedded clauses** (a clause that sits inside a main clause).

 TIP To separate two main clauses in the same sentence without a connective, you need a dash, a colon or a semicolon (see pages 35 to 38).

subordinate clause
↓
As it was raining, I decided to play a board game inside with my sister.
My cousin, **who is nine years older than me,** has just applied for a university course in Chemistry.
↑
embedded clause

4. They can be used with introductory adverbs and **fronted adverbials**. Fronted adverbials are words or phrases that provide information about where, when or how something happens. They are 'fronted' because they are put at the beginning (or 'front') of a sentence.

Cautiously, he tiptoed across the room to avoid being seen.
Fortunately for her, the bus was five minutes later than she was.

5. They separate dialogue from the rest of the text.

"Can anyone tell me," **asked Mrs Conroy,** "what the difference is between a phrase and a clause?"

6. They are used to add in an extra reference to someone or to address someone.

Here, it is already clear which dog is being written about – the name 'Fluffy' is extra information.
↓
My dog, **Fluffy,** loves to play fetch.
"**Amy,** would you please fetch me some more paper?"
↑
Here, 'Amy' is being addressed by the person speaking.

7. They are used with some connectives.

See page 23 for examples of the most common connectives and descriptions of how they are used.

You may be asked to identify where the commas should be in a sentence or passage.

Add the missing commas to the passage.

Nilesh Katherine and Alesha were taking part in the school production of *Oliver*. Since it was Katherine's first time on stage she was feeling quite anxious. Smiling kindly Nilesh reassured her. "Don't worry" he said "you will sing wonderfully."

Look at each sentence and check for any of the features listed on the previous page (lists, clauses, dialogue, extra information or direct addresses to people). Work through the passage slowly, one sentence at a time, and mark in a comma every time you notice that one is missing. For this type of question, you do not need to worry about the punctuation that is already there.

Answer: Nilesh**,** Katherine and Alesha were taking part in the school production of *Oliver*. Since it was Katherine's first time on stage**,** she was feeling quite anxious. Smiling kindly**,** Nilesh reassured her. "Don't worry**,**" he said**,** "you will sing wonderfully."

 Add the missing commas to the passage.

1.   "On your marks get set go!" called out Ms Grover. As the race started Rose zoomed out in front while Jamie followed close behind. They were almost neck and neck. Suddenly Erin who had stumbled at the start appeared and she overtook them both.

You may also be asked to spot places in a passage where commas have been used incorrectly or are missing in a sentence or passage.

Circle any places in the passage where commas have been used incorrectly or are missing.

It was time, to go swimming. Nick who, thought the water was too, cold tried not to show it. Anna, Lucas, and Zara jumped straight in. "Come on" Zara said "it'll warm up, once we get going."

Follow the same procedure as before. Work through the passage and check if commas have been left out. This time you will also need to check every comma that is already in the passage to see if it has been used correctly. Every time you find a mistake, put a circle around the spot that is incorrect.

Answer: It was time(,)to go swimming. Nick(who,)thought the water was too(,)cold tried not to show it. Anna, Lucas(,)and Zara jumped straight in. "Come on(")Zara said(")it'll warm up(,)once we get going."

 Circle any places in the passage where commas have been used incorrectly or are missing.

2.   Although he was an old dog Joe acted like , a puppy. He loved playing fetch for hours he gobbled , down his food in seconds and he tried to sit , in Zack's lap. "Come on , Joe" said Zack "get down! You're far too big for that."

Brackets and dashes

Brackets

Brackets add extra information to a sentence.
They always come in pairs.

> My dog **(a golden retriever)** is very good at tricks.

If you take the information in the brackets away from
the sentence, it still makes sense on its own.

> My dog is very good at tricks.

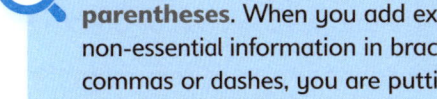

TIP Brackets are sometimes also called **parentheses**. When you add extra, non-essential information in brackets, commas or dashes, you are putting the information in parenthesis.

Brackets can also be used to separate numbers, abbreviations or initialisms from the rest of a sentence.

> Lucy **(13)** is going to be promoted to the first team of Middletown Football Club **(MFC)**.

Make sure you are able to add missing brackets to a sentence.

> Use brackets to separate out the extra information in the sentence.
>
> My birthday 11th October is my favourite day of the entire year.

Look for the extra information that could be taken out without changing the overall meaning of the sentence. In this case, the date of the birthday is not essential information. Make sure that when you put the brackets around that information, the rest of the sentence still makes sense without it.

Answer: My birthday **(11th October)** is my favourite day of the entire year.

 Use brackets to separate out the extra information in each sentence.

1. Jaguars a type of big cat are highly effective predators.

2. My favourite author Roald Dahl wrote more than 30 books.

3. Put your date of birth D.O.B. in the correct format on your passport form.

4. She was too short 99cm to go on the ride.

Dashes

A pair of dashes can also be used to add extra information to a passage. Just like brackets, these go around the extra information to separate it out from the clause around it.

> My cat – a British Short Hair – is very greedy. ← The phrase 'a British Short Hair' tells you the breed of the cat.

Single dashes can also be used to add extra information. They mark a pause in a sentence, often for dramatic effect or to emphasise a point.

> He stopped – somebody was behind the door!
> The sun was shining – not a cloud could be seen in the sapphire sky.

 Single dashes are generally not used in formal writing. Keep them for adding drama to informal writing, and don't use them too often.

Make sure you are able to add missing dashes to a sentence.

> Add the missing dash or dashes to the sentence.
>
> Everyone was very calm until they noticed the tiger creeping up on them!

Look for the natural break or breaks in the sentence. In this case, this is a very dramatic sentence and there is only one break, after the word 'calm'. The sentence needs a single dash added there.

Answer: Everyone was very calm – until they noticed the tiger creeping up on them!

 Add the missing dash or dashes to each sentence.

5. The weather was going to be perfect all day or so we thought.

6. The book that I'm reading *Treasure Island* by Robert Louis Stevenson is about pirates.

7. The school trip a visit to the *Mary Rose* was a huge success.

8. Everything was lovely and peaceful in the house then my little cousin turned up!

Sometimes, you may be asked to spot errors in the use of brackets and dashes.

> Cross out any brackets or dashes that are used incorrectly and add in any that are missing.
>
> Gareth my (cousin) was an excellent swimmer and won lots of medals until – he broke his leg.

First, identify the extra information. At the beginning of the sentence, it isn't just the word 'cousin' – it must include the word 'my' as well, otherwise the rest of the sentence doesn't make sense. At the end of the sentence, the extra information must include the word 'until'. Then think about how the brackets and dashes need to move to show the information correctly.

Answer:

Gareth (my ⁄cousin) was an excellent swimmer and won lots of medals – until ⁄ he broke his leg.

 Cross out any brackets or dashes that are used incorrectly and add in any that are missing.

9. Mr Webb he teaches me maths – is an excellent golfer and has won several trophies.

10. We will be arriving into London (Heathrow) LHR at 3.00 p.m.

11. Vipers a type of (snake) are very poisonous.

12. Andy Murray – a British – tennis player has won Wimbledon twice.

13. The play was about to – start then a member of the audience fainted!

Colons and semicolons

Colons and semicolons may look quite similar, but they are used in different ways. It can be helpful to compare their uses so that you see the differences between them.

Colons

Colons have several different uses. They can be used to introduce items in a list. You only need a colon if the part of the sentence that is not in the list makes sense as a sentence on its own.

'I was shopping for' does not make sense on its own, so this sentence does not need a colon.

I was shopping for two pencils, a pencil sharpener, a notepad and a pen.
I scribbled down my shopping list: two pencils, a pencil sharpener, a notepad and a pen.

'I scribbled down my shopping list' does make sense as a sentence on its own, so this sentence does need a colon.

You might also have seen colons in play **scripts**. They are found between the name of the character and their speech. These colons are not part of a sentence.

Juliet: O Romeo, Romeo, wherefore art thou Romeo?

Colons can also be used to join two main clauses in a sentence when the second one explains the first.

Philippa was so proud of her achievement: she had won an Olympic gold medal.
Mr Green was extremely angry: none of his students had completed their homework.

You may be asked to identify where colons are needed in a sentence.

Add the missing colon to the sentence.

I found my outfit for the tournament a pair of trainers, a white T-shirt, white socks and a pair of red shorts.

First, think about why colons are used. Colons introduce lists or join two main clauses. This sentence has a list of items in an outfit, so the colon will introduce the list. Look for where the list begins. Check that the clause before the list could stand alone as an independent sentence. It could, so you can add the colon immediately before the list.

Answer: I found my outfit for the tournament: a pair of trainers, a white T-shirt, white socks and a pair of red shorts.

 Add the missing colon to each sentence.

1. At 4.00 p.m., the judges' verdict was announced Emilia had won the competition.

2. When he looked in the cage, it dawned upon him the hamster had escaped!

3. Lin purchased the decorations for her party balloons, streamers and banners.

4. On Monday, the drama teacher's choice for the school production was announced the students would perform *Alice in Wonderland*.

5. I had lots of different fruits for breakfast this morning banana, apple, kiwi, pear and mango.

Colons and semicolons

Semicolons

Like colons, semicolons can be used to join two main clauses that are related together in a sentence. Whereas colons join a clause to another clause that explains it, semicolons join two clauses together equally. Neither clause is more important.

Yesterday it was sunny; today it is cloudy.   Soraya likes apples; Will likes oranges.

Semicolons can also be used to separate items in a list when there are many words to describe each item. This provides greater clarity because it makes it easier to see where one item ends and the next begins. If one of the items in the list includes commas, you need to use semicolons to avoid confusion. Unlike commas in a list, you must include a semicolon before the 'and'.

The single list item 'attend art, drama and dance classes' includes commas, so the whole list needs to use semicolons. This will make it easier to read.

In the summer holidays, I like to swim in the sea; climb mountains in Scotland; attend art, drama and dance classes; and compete in tennis tournaments.

You may be asked to identify where a semicolon should go in a sentence or passage.

Add the missing semicolons to the sentence.

At the beach, we saw two yachts three jet-skis five brave, foolish people paddling in the freezing-cold water and one sneaky seagull, which tried to steal our sandwiches.

First, think about why semicolons are used. Semicolons are used between complicated items in a list or to join two equally important clauses. This sentence has a list of complicated items, so you can separate the items with semicolons. Use the nouns to help you make sure that you have identified each item in the list correctly. Remember to add a semicolon before the 'and' introducing the final item.

Answer: At the beach, we saw two yachts; three jet-skis; five brave, foolish people paddling in the freezing-cold water; and one sneaky seagull, which tried to steal our sandwiches.

 Add the missing semicolons to each sentence.

6.   It was a lovely sunny day it seemed as if the whole town had decided to go for a walk.

7.   Nisha received so many presents: a red, yellow and orange pencil case a jumper with a snowman on it a new bell for her bike and a poster of her favourite singer.

8.   Rhys starts school on Tuesday Lacey starts school on Thursday.

9.   At the award ceremony, the actor thanked his agent for getting him fantastic roles to play his mother, who drove him to all his classes as a child his acting coach for all the good advice he gave and his loyal fans.

10. It is important to eat a balanced diet it is also beneficial to exercise regularly.

38

Hyphens

Hyphens are often mistaken for dashes. Their job is to join two words, or a **prefix** and a **root word**, together to create a new idea. They are also used to add clarity to a word or phrase.

There are a few situations in which hyphens may be used.

1. You often need a hyphen to create compound nouns and adjectives. Make sure that you only join together the words that make up one noun or adjective. For example, 'part-time' below is not joined to 'voluntary' because they describe two different attributes of the job (Terry only works sometimes and Terry works for free).

> My little brother wanted another ride on the **merry-go-round**. ← This is a compound noun.
> Terry enjoys his **part-time** voluntary work. ← This is a compound adjective.

> (!) When these adjectives don't come before a noun, they don't need a hyphen. For example, 'Terry enjoys working part time.'

2. To make words clearer to read when they have a prefix. Hyphens might be needed to avoid an awkward letter combination, usually a pair of vowels. They might also be used to stop two similar words looking the same.

> Mason **re-entered** the house after he had said goodbye to his guests.
> When I **recover** from my illness, I will **re-cover** the sofa with velvet.
>
> Here, 'recover' and 're-cover' are two different words.

3. To join tens and units in a number together.

> **forty-two** thousand, six hundred and **seventy-five**

You may be asked to add missing hyphens to a sentence or short passage.

> (TIP) If a word is split over two lines, you can also use a hyphen to show that it is one word.
> She was looking for-ward to the amazing oppor-tunity.

Add the missing hyphen or hyphens to the sentence.

My sister in law gave me an emerald green scarf for my twenty first birthday.

Look through all the rules above and see if any of them apply. Also check if the meaning changes if you add the hyphen.

My sister-in-law gave me an emerald-green scarf for my twenty-first birthday.

compound noun   compound adjective   number

Answer: My sister-in-law gave me an emerald-green scarf for my twenty-first birthday.

 Add the missing hyphen or hyphens to each sentence.

1. The dessert contained mouth watering mango and chocolate covered strawberries.

2. Five hundred and twenty eight people were saved from the deadly avalanche.

3. The election was flawed, so the ex Prime Minister asked for a recount.

4. The car has a state of the art design and is available from mid May.

5. After the freezing cold night, the windscreen had to be de iced.

Apostrophes

Apostrophes have two different functions.

Contraction

They can be used to show that one or more letters have been omitted from a word to shorten it. The apostrophe is placed where the letters have been removed. This is called a contraction.

The 'h' and 'a' from 'have' have been removed.

did n**o**t → didn't   would **ha**ve → would've   it **is** → it's

The 'o' from 'not' has been removed.   The 'i' from 'is' has been removed.

 Write the letter or letters that have been replaced by the apostrophe on the line.

1. I'm _____

2. we're _____

3. haven't _____

4. you'll _____

5. let's _____

6. should've _____

Possession

Apostrophes can also show possession.

If the noun is singular, an apostrophe followed by an 's' is added to the noun.

The cage belonging to the hamster → the hamster**'s** cage.
The pencil case belonging to Julie → Julie**'s** pencil case.
The driver of the bus → the bus**'s** driver.

> (!) If a person's name ends in an 's', the apostrophe can be placed in two ways.
> After the 's': James' pencil (best if you can only hear one 's' sound)
> OR
> After the 's' with an extra 's' added: James's pencil (best if you can hear two 's' sounds, like here)
> Do **not** put the apostrophe before the 's': Jame's pencil.

If more than one person or thing owns the item, then the apostrophe goes after the 's'.

The bowl belonging to the cats → the cats**'** bowl
The toys belonging to the babies → the babies**'** toys

However, if the plural noun does not end in 's', you need to add an apostrophe then 's'.

The classroom of the children → the children**'s** classroom
The team for women → the women**'s** team

 Rewrite the phrase so that it uses an apostrophe to show possession.

7. the jumper belonging to the boy _____

8. the bike belonging to Lois _____

9. the nest belonging to the ants _____

10. the pond belonging to the geese _____

40

Apostrophes

You may be asked to spot errors in the use of apostrophes in a passage, or you may be asked to add apostrophes into a passage where they are needed.

Add the missing apostrophes to the sentence.

Mrs Smiths class couldnt rehearse for their assembly in the school hall as the ladies choir had booked it.

First, look for any words indicating possession. The class belonged to Mrs Smith (a singular proper noun) so her name needs an apostrophe 's' – Mrs Smith**'**s. The choir belonged to the ladies (a plural noun ending in 's'), so it needs an apostrophe after the 's' – ladies**'**.

Finally, look for any contractions. In this sentence, 'could' and 'not' are contracted to make 'couldn**'**t'.

Answer: Mrs Smith**'**s class couldn**'**t rehearse for their assembly in the school hall as the ladies**'** choir had booked it.

! Although you might think that an object belonging to 'it' should end apostrophe 's', remember that 'its' is a pronoun like 'his' and 'her'. You write 'his ball' not 'hi's ball'. Therefore, you write 'the dog fetched its ball' too. Try substituting another pronoun into the sentence and if it still makes sense, you do not need an apostrophe.

 Add the missing apostrophes to each sentence.

11. Its fortunate that warm weather is forecast for the day of the spring picnic.

12. Charles favourite game was chess.

13. I wasnt sure whether six hours would be sufficient to see all the animals in the wildlife park.

14. Isnt it amazing that snakes shed their skin every few months?

15. Sally suddenly realised that shed left her coat at her childrens school.

Here are some of the most common contractions:

it is → it's	I have → I've	it has → it's	does not → doesn't
I am → I'm	have not → haven't	you are → you're	I had → I'd
I will → I'll	would have → would've	will not → won't	let us → let's

Speech marks

Speech marks are punctuation marks that are used to show when someone is speaking. They appear at the beginning and end of **direct speech**. You may also sometimes hear people call speech marks inverted commas – these are two names for the same type of punctuation.

Speech marks are important because they show you exactly which words have been spoken.

It is difficult to see you, I said to Peter, without my glasses on.

Without speech marks, the meaning of this sentence is unclear – did I speak without my glasses on, or am I saying that it is difficult to see without my glasses on?

TIP Speech marks are used to quote the actual words someone speaks. This is called direct speech.

When what someone said is being reported, but the exact words they said are not being used, it is called **indirect speech** or **reported speech**.

With the correct speech punctuation, the meaning becomes clear.

"It is difficult to see you**,"** I said to Peter, **"**without my glasses on.**"**

The speech marks are placed either side of the actual words that are spoken. If the narration continues after the spoken words, a comma is placed before the final speech mark.

"He needs a glass of water**,"** my mother said to my sister.

If the narration starts before the spoken words, a comma goes before the first speech mark.

My mother said to my sister**, "H**e needs a glass of water.**"**

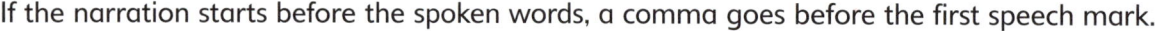

Note here how the actual words spoken start with a capital letter.

Look at what happens if the words spoken are split with some narration between them.

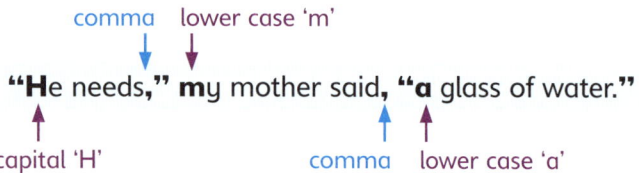

comma   lower case 'm'

"He needs**,"** **m**y mother said**, "a** glass of water.**"**

capital 'H'   comma   lower case 'a'

If the spoken words end with a question mark or an exclamation mark, the rest of the sentence continues in lower case (unless followed by a proper noun).

"Do you need a glass of water**?**" **a**sked my mother.

"Get him a glass of water**!**" **s**houted my mother.

Whenever someone starts speaking, or a new person speaks within a conversation, a new line is used.

"Help!" Dua cried, trying not to fall.
"It's slippery, isn't it?" Caleb called out, grinning as he skated towards her.

It doesn't matter if there is some narration before the speech. You still need to remember the rule, 'new speaker, new line'.

"Please can we make some cookies?" Nadine asked.
Auntie Joy nodded and said, "Chocolate chip or gingerbread?"

A new line is needed because Auntie Joy is about to speak.

Schofield & Sims

Speech marks

Most forms of speech require speech marks. However, there are some cases where speech marks are not used.

Speech marks are only used with direct speech. They quote the actual words someone said. If you are not quoting the exact words spoken, you do not need speech marks.

This is direct speech because it is the exact words Mum spoke. It needs speech marks.

"**Can I have a glass of water**?" asked Mum.
My mother asked **if she could have a glass of water**.

 TIP See page 44 for more on reported speech.

Someone else is telling us what Mum said in their own words, so this is reported speech. It does not need speech marks.

Speech marks are also not used in speech bubbles or play scripts. They are not needed in speech bubbles because the bubble indicates who is saying what. In play scripts, the layout is used to show who is speaking and what they are saying. The speaker is followed by a colon and then their speech.

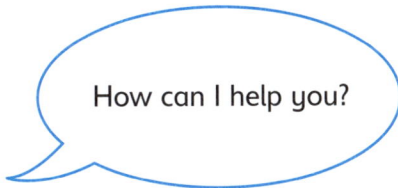
How can I help you?

Mary: How long do we have to wait?

Connor: Until the clock strikes 12.

When speech marks are missing from a sentence or paragraph, you may be asked to add them in. If you notice any other missing punctuation, you can add that in as well. You will also need to show where there should be new paragraphs if those are missing.

> Rewrite the passage, adding the correct speech punctuation.
>
> Where are you shouted Claire. She was looking for Jack while playing hide-and-seek but couldn't find him and was starting to worry. He replied Over here. Why can't you see me? As hard as she looked, he remained invisible to her. No matter how loudly you shout she remarked, I can't see you!

Decide which words you think are actually being spoken by the characters and put speech marks around them. Put either a comma, question mark or an exclamation mark before the final speech mark if the sentence continues. If it does not, add a full stop. Look at where other commas are needed to separate the speech from the rest of the sentence. Each time a new person begins talking, start a new line.

> **Answer:** "Where are you**?**" shouted Claire. She was looking for Jack while playing hide-and-seek but couldn't find him and was starting to worry.
>
> He replied**,** "Over here. Why can't you see me?"
>
> As hard as she looked, he remained invisible to her.
>
> "No matter how loudly you shout**,**" she remarked, "I can't see you!"

 Rewrite the passage, adding the correct speech punctuation.

1.   It was time for the weekly multiplication test. Who asked Mrs Taylor can tell me what the product of 7 and 8 is Everyone looked bewildered. I don't know what a product is said Angel bravely I've never heard that word before. Kwame piped up cheerfully I know what it is It is when you multiply one number with another number he announced confidently.

Direct speech and reported speech

As explained on page 42, speech marks are used to quote the actual words someone speaks. This is called direct speech.

When what someone said is being reported, but the exact words they said are not being used, it is called indirect speech or reported speech.

You may be asked to change reported speech into direct speech, or vice versa.

Turn this direct speech into reported speech.

"I need a new toothbrush," Chioma told the dentist.

TIP Indirect speech often includes words like 'that' or 'if'.

To convert this direct speech into reported speech, the words spoken by Chioma need to be changed from the present tense into the past tense, and the first person pronoun 'I' needs to be changed into the third person pronoun 'she'.

Answer: Chioma told the dentist that she needed a new toothbrush.

TIP For more on using the first, second and third person in your writing, see page 101.

Reverse the process when changing reported speech into direct speech.

Mrs Hughes said that, at one time, everyone thought the sun revolved around the earth.
"At one time, everyone thought the sun revolved around the earth**," said Mrs Hughes.**

Remember to add the comma.
Include speech marks.
Add who is speaking at the end.

Turn this direct speech into reported speech.

1. "It is late. I need to catch my bus," said Flavia.

_____

2. Shivesh said, "No matter how hard I try, I cannot play tennis very well."

_____

3. "If you all work hard," claimed Mr Spencer, "you will succeed."

_____

Turn this reported speech into direct speech.

4. Daisy asked if she could join the football club after Christmas.

_____

5. Aaron noticed that it was getting very dark outside and that it might rain.

_____

6. Veronica asked Tiana when her birthday was.

_____

Punctuation practice page 1

Now test your skills with these practice pages. If you get stuck, go back to pages 30 to 44 for some reminders.

Sentence punctuation

Circle the punctuation mistakes in each sentence.

1.   I am reading a very exciting book at the moment called swallows and amazons.

2.   Is the start of the holidays today or tomorrow!

3.   That is an amazing test score – well done?

4.   I am hoping that I can finish my homework quickly It is my birthday tomorrow.

Circle the letter of the sentence that is punctuated correctly.

5.   **A.**   Is buckingham palace open today?

     B.   is Buckingham Palace open today?

     C.   Is Buckingham Palace open today.

     D.   Is Buckingham Palace open today?

6.   **A.**   There in ... the bath was a spider!

     B.   There in the ... bath was a spider!

     C.   There in the bath was ... a spider!

     D.   There in the bath was a spider ... !

Commas

Add the missing commas to each sentence.

7.   Anxiously the waiter carried the soup out hoping not to spill it.

8.   "Lily-Mae I hope that you can come to my party next week."

9.   Without any warning the hurricane changed course and swept into Florida.

Circle any places in each sentence where commas have been used incorrectly or are missing.

10.   I need to buy , a fountain pen , colouring pencils , and a selection of paints.

11.   Deep , in the dark gloomy forest stood a tall towering tree.

12.   Reluctantly she realised , that she would have to admit defeat.

13.   "I wish " , she moaned , "that I was just a little , bit taller!"

Brackets and dashes

Use brackets to separate out the extra information in each sentence.

1. Chameleons famous for camouflaging themselves can be found living in the rainforests of Madagascar.
2. The puppy 21 weeks old was found hiding behind a neighbour's toolshed.
3. Please reply ASAP as soon as possible in order to get your tickets.
4. Diwali the festival of light is celebrated in either October or November.

Add the missing dash or dashes to each sentence.

5. Everyone thought the tiger had been captured except the zookeeper!
6. All students including sixth-formers must attend school in uniform.
7. The sky was pitch-black not a star could be seen for miles.
8. Tasmania an island off the south coast of Australia is known for its many exotic creatures, such as the Tasmanian devil.

Cross out any brackets or dashes that are used incorrectly and add in any that are missing.

9. My older sister Louise) has just trained as a yoga (teacher.
10. I cannot believe – it I have seen four lightning strikes in a row.
11. We made a birthday cake (chocolate) fudge for my party.
12. The juggler threw – seven balls in the air then dropped them all!
13. My – pet dog – named Buster is going to be twelve years old – soon.
14. It is very worthwhile learning) to play an instrument especially the drums or piano as it helps develop co-ordination.

Colons and semicolons

Add the missing colon to each sentence.

15. The results were revealed in reverse order Jian had received third prize.
16. It wasn't long before he realised his mistake he had taken the wrong turn at the last junction.
17. On Monday morning, the classroom was sweltering somebody had left the radiator on over the weekend.

Add the missing semicolons to each sentence.

18. The atmosphere was tense nobody wanted to leave the auditorium in case they missed hearing who had won.
19. It is very hard to learn another language some people try for years.
20. On holiday, I would like to try snorkelling with turtles whale watching in a glass-bottomed boat sailing and perhaps surfing as well.
21. It was a beautiful day everyone was enjoying the unusually warm weather.

Hyphens

Add the missing hyphen or hyphens to each sentence.

1. The record breaking athlete trained extremely hard every day.

2. Sixty seven people from our town joined the protest on Saturday.

3. The space shuttle vibrated violently on re entry to Earth's atmosphere.

4. The first few years in post apartheid South Africa were a time of great hope.

5. Heather's gift was a beautiful, satin lined coat.

6. The president elect will not take office until mid January.

7. As the actor thought about the ninety seven people in the audience, he was suddenly stricken with fright.

8. Lots of well known rock bands became famous in the 1960s.

9. "That sofa is so filthy! It definitely needs re covering."

10. My new flat has a well equipped kitchen with lots of modern gadgets.

Apostrophes

Add the missing apostrophes to each sentence.

11. It doesnt feel like winter as the weather is so warm!

12. I am hoping that the parents evening wont last too long as I am starving!

13. Willas favourite animal is her pet rabbit because its fur is so soft.

14. The childrens party at my house is going to be very chaotic – I will need everyones help.

15. Its cute when the excited dog wags its tail expectantly, hoping for a large, juicy bone.

16. Most cakes contain cows milk and other dairy produce.

17. The babies toys were scattered all over the floor, but their parents werent the least bit concerned.

18. He walks his own dog every day but doesnt ever notice any other dogs in the park.

19. I wont go to netball practice today as theyre only practising passing and I prefer shooting.

20. The womens rugby team hasnt lost a game in two seasons!

Speech marks

Rewrite the sentences, adding the correct speech punctuation.

1. Do you think said Chloe that the interview is here?

    "Do you think" Said chloe "that the interveiw is here?"

2. Can I come in and look at your new piano asked Ivan

    _____

3. Don't go near the water as there are lots of jellyfish shouted Naomi

    _____

4. Aunty Marion said come here, I want to see how much you have grown

    _____

5. Can I check asked Danielle whether that's my jumper

    _____

6. Run shouted Mark The dog is after us

    _____

Direct speech and reported speech

Turn this direct speech into reported speech.

7. "I'm ever so sorry to hear that you have been unwell," Alys said to Jerome.

    _____

8. "Wouldn't it be great," Deborah said with a smile, "if we won the lottery this weekend."

    _____

9. "Don't forget to bring a packed lunch for the trip!" Mr Patel shouted to the children.

    _____

Turn this reported speech into direct speech.

10. Ms Davis told the class not to leave the room without her permission.

    _____

11. An eyewitness remarked that the queue was so long that she couldn't see the end.

    _____

12. A spectator said that it was a very enjoyable concert, although it was too loud.

    _____

Singular and plural words

There are several rules for converting singular words into plural words that you need to be aware of.

1. To make most nouns plural, you just add **s** at the end:

    cat → cat**s**   pen → pen**s**   printer → printer**s**   window → window**s**

    radiator → radiator**s**

2. However, you need to add **es** to words ending in **s**, **x**, **z**, **ch** or **sh**. These words often gain an extra syllable when they become plural:

    dre**ss** → dre**sses**   bo**x** → bo**xes**   qui**z** → qui**zzes**   wit**ch** → wit**ches**   bu**sh** → bu**shes**

3. If a word ends in **y** after a consonant, drop the **y** and add **ies**:

    cr**y** → cr**ies**   bab**y** → bab**ies**   sp**y** → sp**ies**

    However, if there is a vowel before the **y**, just add **s**:

    donke**y** → donke**ys**   Monda**y** → Monda**ys**   ke**y** → ke**ys**

    > **TIP** Consonants are all the letters apart from **a**, **e**, **i**, **o** and **u**. These letters are vowels.

4. Add **ves** to words that end in **f** or **fe**:

    wol**f** → wol**ves**   scar**f** → scar**ves**   thie**f** → thie**ves**

    However, there are some important exceptions that just need an **s**. These include all words that end in **ff** and a few words that end in a single **f** that you will need to learn.

    sni**ff** → sni**ffs**   oa**f** → oa**fs**   belie**f** → belie**fs**   chie**f** → chie**fs**   roo**f** → roo**fs**

5. Add **es** if the word ends in **o**:

    ech**o** → ech**oes**   her**o** → her**oes**   volcan**o** → volcan**oes**

    However, if it is a musical, foreign or shortened word, you usually just add **s**:

    pian**o** → pian**os**   sol**o** → sol**os**   kil**o** → kil**os**   rhin**o** → rhin**os**   phot**o** → phot**os**

6. Words with a Greek or Latin origin have their own rules, depending on the word endings:

is → es	**us → i**	**a → ae**
diagnos**is** → diagnos**es**	stimul**us** → stimul**i**	larv**a** → larv**ae**
um → a	**on → a**	**ix → ices**
referend**um** → referend**a**	phenomen**on** → phenomen**a**	matr**ix** → matr**ices**

7. In some cases, the plural form of the word is exactly the same as the singular form:

    deer → deer   sheep → sheep   moose → moose

8. Some irregular plurals do not follow a particular rule. You just have to learn these exceptions:

    child → children   man → men   woman → women   mouse → mice

    person → people   foot → feet   goose → geese

> ⚠ **Dice** is not singular – it is the plural of **die**.
> A **compass** is an instrument you use to find the right direction. A **pair of compasses** is the instrument you use to draw circles.

Singular and plural words

You may be asked to choose the correct plurals to complete a sentence or to write the plural form of a word given in brackets.

Underline the correct plural of the words that complete the sentence.

My *heroes / heros / heroies* have all triumphed over many personal *tragedeys / tragedys / tragedies*.

Look at the options for each plural in turn and think about the correct spelling rule. Watch out for the exceptions. 'Hero' ends in 'o', so needs –es added to the end. As 'tragedy' ends in a consonant followed by 'y', you need to drop the 'y' and add –ies.

Answer: My <u>heroes</u> / *heros* / *heroies* have all triumphed over many personal *tragedeys / tragedys / <u>tragedies</u>*.

Use the correct plural of the word in brackets to complete the sentence.

There were hundreds of _____ (person) in the crowd.

As before, think about what spelling rules could apply to this word. In this case, 'person' is a word with an irregular plural. You must learn that the plural of 'person' is 'people'.

Answer: There were hundreds of **people** (person) in the crowd.

> ! You never use an apostrophe to make a word plural. Apostrophes are only used with nouns in the possessive form.
> For example, **a large bowl of raspberry's** is incorrect. It should be **a large bowl of raspberries**.
> **The raspberries' packaging was eco-friendly** is correct.

Underline the correct plural of the word that completes each sentence.

1. The football team for *womans* / <u>women</u> / *woman* are having a very successful season.

2. We learn to use *knifs* / *knive's* / <u>knives</u> safely in cookery class.

3. There are lots of damaged <u>trolleys</u> / *trolles* / *trollys* in the supermarket car park.

4. We need more <u>cellos</u> / *celloies* / *cello's* in the string section of our orchestra.

Use the correct plural of the word in brackets to complete each sentence.

5. We get a lot of ___foxes___ (fox) in my garden.

6. The river was full of jumping ___fish___ (fish).

7. The rubbish was left out so long that it attracted a multitude of ___flies___ (fly).

8. I dislike ~~tomato~~ tomatoes (tomato), so I always pick them out of my salad.

Root words, prefixes and suffixes

Prefix

A prefix is a string of letters added to the start of a word to make a new word. The word that you add the prefix to is called the root word.

For example, the prefix un– is added to the start of the root word 'happy' to create the word 'unhappy', meaning 'not happy' (sad).

 TIP Prefixes and suffixes are both types of **affix**. An affix is a part added to the beginning or end of a word.

There are many prefixes and they have specific meanings. Some of the most common prefixes and their meanings are included in the table below. An example of a word that uses each prefix is given in brackets.

ante – before (**ante**room)	**re** – again (**re**-do)	**semi** – half (**semi**-final)
co – together (**co**-operate)	**sub** – under (**sub**marine)	**auto** – by itself (**auto**matic)
ex – former (**ex**-colleague)	**trans** – across (**trans**atlantic)	**circum** – around (**circum**ference)
inter – between (**inter**national)	**pre** – before (**pre**historic)	**fore** – before (**fore**cast)
post – after (**post**game)	**tele** – far off/distant (**tele**phone)	**micro** – small (**micro**scope)
omni – everything (**omni**vore)	**uni/bi/tri/quad** – 1/2/3/4 (**uni**verse, **bi**cycle, **tri**pod, **quad**rilateral)	**thermo** – heat (**thermo**meter)
super – above (**super**impose)	**out** – further/better than (**out**do)	**hyper** – over (**hyper**ventilate)

Some prefixes are used to make a word that means the opposite of the root word.

anti – against (**anti**clockwise)	**im** – not (**im**mature)	**mis** – not (**mis**behave)
contra – against (**contra**diction)	**dis** – the opposite (**dis**appear)	**ir** – not (**ir**replaceable)
il – not (**il**legal)	**un** – not (**un**able)	**in** – not (**in**dependent)

Prefixes can sometimes be hyphenated when they are added to the root word. This can be for several reasons. It might be because the first letter of the root word is the same as the last letter of the prefix. For example:

re-enter   co-ordinate   pre-eminent

It could be to prevent confusion if there is another word that looks similar but has a different meaning. For example:

re-press (to press again)   repress (to hold something back)

Finally, there are some prefixes that are almost always hyphenated. These are **self-**, **all-**, **ex-** and **mid-**. For example:

self-centred   all-powerful   ex-police officer   mid-sentence

Suffix

A suffix is a string of letters added to the end of a root word to alter its meaning.

For example, the suffix –ful is added to the end of the root word 'help' to create the word 'helpful'.

TIP The suffix –cian usually refers to occupations – **magician**, **clinician**, **mathematician**, **electrician**, **statistician** and so on.

 The suffix –ful is often confused with the word 'full' and spelt with a double 'l'. It only becomes a double 'l' if –ly is added after it. For example, grate**ful** → grate**fully**.

Here is a table of common suffixes.

ed: turn – turn**ed**	**est**: small – small**est**	**less**: hope – hope**less**	**able/ible**: comfort – comfort**able**
en: gold – gold**en**	**ity**: moral – moral**ity**	**ing**: jump – jump**ing**	**sion**: confuse – confu**sion**
ly: sad – sad**ly**	**ness**: kind – kind**ness**	**ment**: move – move**ment**	**cian**: magic – magi**cian**
ful: tear – tear**ful**	**er**: teach – teach**er**	**tion**: inform – informa**tion**	**ous**: poison – poison**ous**

There are specific spelling rules to keep in mind when adding suffixes to root words.

1. Double the final consonant if the last syllable of the word is stressed and ends with only one consonant and a vowel before it.

    ho**p** → ho**pping**/ho**pped**   prefer → prefe**rring**/prefe**rred**   cla**p** → cla**pping**/cla**pped**

    If the last syllable is not stressed, or if the word ends with two consonants or two vowels before the last consonant, do not double the final letter. The letter **x** is never doubled.

    prefer → prefer**able**   ju**mp** → ju**mping**   s**oar** → s**oared**   fi**x** → fi**xing**

2. When adding suffixes beginning with a vowel to words ending in **e**, drop the **e** before adding the suffix. When the **e** is after a **c** or a **g**, to create a soft sound as in 'change', do not drop the **e**.

    hop**e** → hop**ing**   shin**e** → shin**y**   defin**e** → defin**able**   notic**e** → notic**eable**

3. When adding a suffix to a word ending in a consonant followed by **y**, drop the **y** and replace it with an **i** before adding the suffix.

    gloom**y** → gloom**ily**/gloom**iest**   fur**y** → fur**ious**   carr**y** → carr**ied**/carr**ies**

    However, when adding **–ing**, the **y** remains.

    cr**y** → cr**ying**   rel**y** → rel**ying**   stud**y** → stud**ying**

4. If a word ends with **–our**, it is changed to **or** before adding **–ous**.

    glam**our** → glam**orous**   hum**our** → hum**orous**

 The word 'mischievous' (mis-cheev-ous) is often misspelt because it is pronounced incorrectly (mis-cheev-ee-ous). To add –ous, remove the 'f' from 'mischief' and replace it with a 'v', then add –ous: mischievous.

Root words, prefixes and suffixes

You may be asked to spot spelling mistakes involving prefixes and suffixes.

Underline the prefix or suffix which has been used incorrectly and then write out the correct version on the line.

It was inpossible to see due to the lack of streetlights in the town centre. _____

Look for any words with prefixes and suffixes. Check to see if they have been used correctly.

Put a tick above them if they have and underline them if they haven't. In this passage, the only word with a prefix is 'inpossible'. While in– is a prefix meaning 'not', this prefix should be im– when it appears before 'p'. Underline 'inpossible' and write out the correct form on the line.

Answer: It was <u>in</u>possible to see due to the lack of streetlights in the town centre.   **impossible**

Underline the prefixes and suffixes which have been used incorrectly and then write out the correct version on the line.

1.   I am so gratement for the help that I have received.   _____

2.   It was imfortunate that I lost my keys on the train.   _____

3.   I disjudged how long the cake needed to bake.   _____

4.   My new kittens are so cuddly and lovible.   _____

5.   One superordinary day, a surprise visitor came to school.   _____

6.   The weather was very changeable – sun then torrencial rain.   _____

You may be asked to choose the correct prefix or suffix to complete a word in a sentence or paragraph.

Add the correct prefix or suffix to the word in brackets to complete the sentences.

Pandas are such _____ (adore) creatures. They were certainly the _____ (cute) animals at the zoo. It was _____ (fortunate) that they were asleep for most of our visit, but they woke up right at the end.

Look at whether it is a prefix or suffix (or both) that you need to include for the word to make sense in the passage. If it is a suffix you need to add, look at the rest of the passage to make sure the grammar agrees with the other words.

The word 'adore' needs a suffix to say what the pandas are like. –able works. The 'e' must be dropped. The word 'cute' needs a suffix meaning 'the most'. –est works. Since 'cute' already ends with 'e', add 'st' to the end. The word 'fortunate' could fit in the sentence. However, the person was upset that the pandas were asleep. A prefix meaning 'the opposite' will work best.

Answer: Pandas are such **adorable** creatures. They were certainly the **cutest** animals at the zoo. It was **unfortunate** that they were asleep for most of our visit, but they woke up right at the end.

Root words, prefixes and suffixes

Add the correct prefix or suffix to the word in brackets to complete each sentence.

7. Our class are the most _____ (study) group of students in the whole school.

8. For many isolated people, _____ (lonely) is a real concern.

9. You must _____ (frost) the meat well before cooking it.

10. The kitten ventured _____ (curious) into the garden.

11. I couldn't _____ (see) what was going to happen next, but I hoped it would be exciting.

12. After the excitement of the holidays, I was looking forward to getting back to _____ (normal).

Root words

Root words are the words you begin with before you add any prefixes or suffixes. Make sure you can identify the root word from a longer word.

Write the root word for each of these words.

unhelpful   unemployed   laziness

Look for all the prefixes and suffixes in the word and cross them out. You will then be left with the root word. You may need to change some of the letters back to what they would have been before a suffix had been added.

~~un~~help~~ful~~ = help

~~un~~employ~~ed~~ = employ

lazi~~ness~~ = lazy

Answer: help   employ   lazy

> **TIP** A **word family** is all the words related to one root word. For example, **use, useful, useless, reuse, reusable** and **misuse** are all related to the root word **use**.

Write the root word for each of these words.

13. comfortable _____

14. reheated _____

15. underappreciated _____

16. hurriedly _____

17. unfaithful _____

18. precooking _____

19. transplanted _____

20. dissatisfied _____

> ! The spelling of the root word may have changed slightly when the affix was added.

Homophones

Homophones are words that sound the same but have different spellings and different meanings. For example, 'hair' and 'hare' are homophones.

I need a new brush as this one tangles my **hair**.
If you look over there, you will see a **hare** running across the field.

Some common homophones are easily confused.

TIP To remember which spelling goes with which meaning for the homophones stationery/ stationary, think 'e' is for 'envelope'. Then you will link it to 'stationery' meaning items to do with paper and pens.

Whose coat has been handed in to lost property? ← This is a possessive pronoun.
Who's going to be elected as Class Captain this year? ← This is a contraction meaning 'who is'.

I am going **to** the cinema tonight. ← This is a preposition.
This homework on algebra is **too** difficult for me. ← This is an adverb.
Look at the **two** ducks waddling across the playground! ← This is a number.

Over **there** you will see a beautiful statue of Queen Victoria. ← This is an adverb.
Their newborn twins are amazingly quiet during the night. ← This is a possessive pronoun.
I hope **they're** not too late! ← This is a contraction meaning 'they are'.

 Homophones are not to be confused with **homonyms**. Homonyms are words which have the same spelling but a different meaning. Homonyms will be covered in more detail on page 69.

You might be given a definition of a homophone and asked to give the correct spelling of the word or you may be asked to choose the correct homophone to complete a sentence.

Write the correct word with the correct spelling for each meaning. The first letter of each word has been given to help you.

a person who attends an event or party   **G** _____

Think of some words that fit the definition. This could be a 'visitor' or a 'guest'. 'Guest' begins with 'G', so this might be the answer. Check that you can think of a homophone for 'guest'. In this case, the past tense of 'guess' – 'guessed' – would be a homophone, so 'guest' must be the answer.

Answer: guest

 Write the correct word with the correct spelling for each meaning. The first letter of each word has been given to help you.

1. given permission to do something   **A** _____

2. someone who foretells the future   **P** _____

3. entire and complete   **W** _____

Underline the correct homophones of the words that complete each sentence.

4. A ravenous eagle circled *hire / higher* above its *prey / pray* before swooping down to catch it.

5. The berry tasted *sweet / suite* and was full of sticky *red / read* juice.

6. The *fair / fare* for the bus has increased *to / too* much in recent years.

Spot spelling mistakes

It is essential that you are able to spell accurately, and that you can spot spelling mistakes in texts.

You will already have learnt many spellings in school. However, it is a good idea to revise the most important spelling rules and to be aware of the most common spelling errors.

Silent letters

A silent letter is a letter that is included in the spelling of a word but has no sound when you pronounce the word. You need to be careful when spelling words containing silent letters because simply sounding them out will not tell you how to spell them.

The most common silent letters, and some examples of words they appear in, are in the table below.

silent **b**	lam**b**, lim**b**, com**b**, thum**b**, de**b**t, dou**b**t
silent **c**	s**c**ented, s**c**ience, s**c**issors, as**c**end, ya**c**ht
silent **d**	han**d**some, We**d**nesday, we**d**ge, han**d**kerchief
silent **g**	si**g**n, forei**g**n, mali**g**n, desi**g**n, fei**g**n
silent **h**	w**h**ich, w**h**ere, w**h**y, w**h**at, c**h**oir, ec**h**o, sc**h**ool, g**h**ostly, ag**h**ast, spag**h**etti
silent **k**	**k**night, **k**nife, **k**now, **k**nock, **k**nee, **k**nead
silent **l**	sa**l**mon, ca**l**m, shou**l**d, wou**l**d, yo**l**k, cha**l**k
silent **n**	autum**n**, hym**n**, solem**n**, colum**n**
silent **s**	i**s**land, i**s**le, ai**s**le
silent **t**	wi**t**ch, wa**t**ch, lis**t**en, cas**t**le, balle**t**, gourme**t**
silent **u**	bisc**u**it, b**u**ild, g**u**itar, g**u**ess, g**u**ardian
silent **w**	**w**rite, **w**rong, **w**restle, **w**ho, **w**hole, ans**w**er, t**w**o

Double consonants

Words often contain a mixture of single and double consonants. Knowing when to use double consonants can be tricky, but there are some rules you can use to help you remember.

1. Double consonants often come before or after short vowel sounds in words.

acco**mm**odation   a**dd**ress   emba**rr**assing   fulfi**ll**   posse**ss**ive

esse**nt**ial   tomo**rr**ow   bro**cc**oli   disa**pp**ointing   di**ff**erent

o**cc**asional   para**ll**el   su**cc**essful   i**mm**ediate

2. Double consonants often come before –le endings in words.

pa**dd**le   bu**bb**le   sa**dd**le   gi**gg**le   squa**bb**le

befu**dd**le   dri**bb**le   qui**bb**le   stu**bb**le

3. Double consonants often come before the suffixes –ing, –ed, –y or –er in words with short vowel sounds before the final consonant.

cram → cra**mm**ed, cra**mm**ing

slip → sli**pp**ed, sli**pp**ing, sli**pp**y, sli**pp**er

run → ru**nn**ing, ru**nn**y, ru**nn**er

> **!** The prefix dis– is often written with a double 's' as 'dissappear'. This is incorrect. It should always be a single 's' unless the root word begins with 's'. For example, **disappear**, **dissatisfied**.

Schofield & Sims

Spot spelling mistakes

Unstressed vowels

Sometimes, a vowel in a word is not pronounced clearly, so it is difficult to work out just from listening to it exactly which vowel it is. This can make spelling these words especially tricky.

> def**i**nitely – the second **i** is pronounced as 'uh' so the word is often misspelt as 'definately'
> occurr**e**nce – the first **e** is pronounced 'uh' so the word is often misspelt as 'occurance'

Sometimes, the vowel sound is omitted from the spoken word altogether.

> diff**e**rent – the first **e** is omitted so the word is often misspelt as 'diffrent'
> mis**e**rable – the first **e** is omitted so the word is often misspelt as 'misrable'

Other commonly misspelt words with unstressed vowels include **calendar** (pronounced calender), **parliament** (pronounced parliment), **interest** (pronounced intrest), **manage** (pronounced manige) and **restaurant** (pronounced restront).

The 'i' before 'e' rule

People often confuse the order of these two letters within words. However, there is a simple rhyme you can learn to help you remember the correct order:

> **i** before **e** except after **c**,
>
> and only when the word rhymes with **see**

In other words, the word must contain the long 'ee' sound. These words do contain the long 'ee' sound, and do not have a 'c' immediately before it, so they are 'ie' spellings:

f**ie**ld   bel**ie**ve   th**ie**f

sh**ie**ld   pr**ie**st   retr**ie**ve

Even though these words contain the long 'ee' sound, they also contain 'c' immediately before it, so they are 'ei' spellings:

c**ei**ling   rec**ei**pt   dec**ei**ve

conc**ei**ted   perc**ei**ve   conc**ei**ve

Where there is neither a 'c' nor a long 'ee' sound, words are spelt with an 'ei':

n**ei**ghbour   **ei**ght   w**ei**ght   l**ei**sure   b**ei**ge   for**ei**gn

h**ei**st   th**ei**r   h**ei**r   forf**ei**t   h**ei**ght   n**ei**ther

Where there is a 'c' but the sound after it is not the long 'ee' the spelling may be 'ie':

sc**ie**nce   consc**ie**nce   effic**ie**nt   suffic**ie**nt

 There are still some exceptions to these rules, such as 'protein' and 'fancied'. You will need to learn how to spell these words as you come across them.

Verbs and nouns with –ise and –ice

There are some verbs and nouns that sound the same but are spelt differently. The verbs end in –ise and the nouns end in –ice.

You will need to think carefully about whether you are using a verb or a noun when you are writing to make sure you are using the right spelling. Thinking about the subject, verb and object in the sentence can help you choose the correct spelling.

Here are some of the most common examples.

Verb

practise – Olamide **practises** her clarinet at lunchtime.
advise – I would **advise** you to revise for thirty minutes a day.
devise – The police **devised** a clever plan to catch the thief.

Noun

practice – Hockey **practice** was cancelled last Friday.
advice – The **advice** I would give you is to study hard.
device – The **device** controlled all the lights in the building.

Other commonly confused words

Sometimes, two words are similar but spelt differently, affecting the meaning and pronunciation.

affect – **e**ffect

The cold weather will **affect** the conditions on the playing field.
The **effect** of the cold weather on driving conditions is very dangerous.

Affect is a verb. **Effect** is a noun.

accept – **ex**cept

Please **accept** my apologies for being late.
I go to the beach every weekend **except** if it's raining.

Accept is a verb. **Except** is a conjunction.

de**s**ert – de**ss**ert

The **desert** has seen no rain in over two years.
The **dessert** of the day is chocolate crunch cake.

Desert is a noun. **Dessert** is also a noun, but it has a different meaning and pronunciation.

Pacific – **spe**cific

The **Pacific** is the largest of the oceans.
Be **specific** when you answer the questions.

Pacific is a proper noun. **Specific** is an adjective.

 TIP Many other commonly confused words are homophones. See page 55 for some homophones you are likely to come across.

 There isn't a single rule to learn for commonly confused words. Instead, you will need to practise any words you come across. Learning them in a sentence can help you remember their meaning.

Schofield & Sims

Spot spelling mistakes

You may be asked to spot spelling mistakes in a sentence or short passage.

Underline the spelling mistakes in the passage and then write out the misspelt words with the correct spelling.

The accomodation is completely inadequeate. This was meant to be a specal occassion, but it has been ruined by dirty curtans and a lumpy bed. I am gratefull that my cusin has a spare bed in her hotel room, but I will have to wait until tommorrow to move in, which is dissappointing.

Read through the passage, looking out particularly for words containing silent letters, single and double consonants, unstressed vowels, 'ie' or 'ei' letter combinations and commonly mistaken words. Also look for mistakes where prefixes or suffixes have been added.

Answer:

The accomodation (**accommodation**) is completely inadequeate (**inadequate**). This was meant to be a specal (**special**) occassion (**occasion**), but it has been ruined by dirty curtans (**curtains**) and a lumpy bed. I am gratefull (**grateful**) that my cusin (**cousin**) has a spare bed in her hotel room, but I will have to wait until tommorrow (**tomorrow**) to move in, which is dissappointing (**disappointing**).

 Underline the spelling mistake in each sentence and then write out the misspelt word with the correct spelling.

1. The painting was an origanal by Monet and was considered priceless.　　　_origanal_ ✓

2. Roaring fearcely, the lion ran away from the poachers.　　　_fearcly_ ✗

3. The dessert was surprisingly cool at night.　✗　_desert_　R surprising? ✗

4. They decided to seperate the players into an A team and a B team.　　　_separate_ ✓

5. A freind of mine was just saying how much fun playing tennis is.　　　_friend_ ✓

6. Jacob's online busness was becoming very successful.　　　_business_ ✓

Underline the correct spelling of the word that completes each sentence.

7. A *squirell* / *squirel* / *squirrel* scampered across the roof and into the oak tree.

8. Did you hear that *wierd* / *weird* / *weerd* noise a moment ago?

9. The more I *practice* / *practise* / *praktice*, the better I will be.

10. When I returned the clothes, the cashier asked for my *receipt* / *reciebt* / *receit*.

Now test your skills with these practice pages. If you get stuck, go back to pages 49 to 59 for some reminders.

Singular and plural

Underline the correct plural of the word that completes each sentence.

1. How many *loafs / loavs / loaves* of bread are there in the oven?

2. This soup contains *potatos / potatoes / potatows*, carrots, peas and leeks.

3. The *witches / witchis / whiches* cackled menacingly as they gathered around the cauldron.

4. The chefs had lots of spices on their *shelfes / shelves / shelvs*.

5. I can hear *mouses / mices / mice* scuttling around in the attic.

6. The farmer brought his *sheep / sheeps / sheepes* into the barn for the winter.

7. Our resort is the ideal holiday destination for *families / familys / family's*.

8. The chimney sweep paused for a moment to look out over the *roofes / roovs / roofs*.

Use the correct plural of the word in brackets to complete each sentence.

9. Shakespeare's plays include many _____ (tragedy).

10. My _____ (tooth) need examining by the dentist.

11. The exam gave her several _____ (stimulus) to choose from.

12. Look at all those _____ (donkey) roaming around that field.

13. She couldn't decide which one of the beautiful _____ (scarf)

    she wanted.

14. I put down all my _____ (domino) first, so I won the round.

Root words, prefixes and suffixes

Underline the prefixes and suffixes which have been used incorrectly and then write out the correct version on the line.

1. It was very antiresponsible of you to walk across that busy road.   _____

2. I had to overheat the oven before I put the cake inside.   _____

3. The fairy lights added a magicful touch to the room.   _____

4. Sorry, but I disunderstood the question.   _____

5. Everyone else was very excited about the trip, but Sammy

    was imdifferent.   _____

6. She was the youngous girl in the class by two months.   _____

7. We had to call the electritian as all the lights went out.   _____

8. Henna was grateness for the help she got with tidying the classroom.   _____

9. He was perfectly capible of completing his homework, but he refused.   _____

Add the correct prefix or suffix to the word in brackets to complete each sentence.

10. The judge commented that the thief had been very   _____   (honest).

11. The   _____   (marine) descended when enemy boats came into sight.

12. "Make yourself   _____   (comfort) while I finish cooking dinner," Hayden said.

13. Yasmin is very   _____   (differ) from her sister.

14. The highly   _____   (combust) fabric burst into flames.

15. She turned and walked away in the other   _____   (direct).

16. An important   _____   (national) football match is taking place this Saturday.

17. The doctor's surgery is aiming to   _____   (computer) all its medical records.

Write the root word for each of these words.

18. musician   _____

19. indecision   _____

20. terrify   _____

21. disconnected   _____

22. thankfulness   _____

23. encouragement   _____

Homophones

Write the correct word with the correct spelling for each meaning. The first letter of each word has been given to help you.

1. a mammal similar to a rabbit but larger H _____

2. the bottom of your foot or shoe S _____

3. a religious song heard in church H _____

4. the person who inherits something H _____

5. a food you eat for breakfast with milk C _____

6. the pleasant aroma a flower gives off S _____

7. having a rough texture C _____

8. to pull something along with a rope T _____

Underline the correct homophones of the words that complete each sentence.

9. "Dad's ice cream van *past / passed* the MOT!" shrieked Paula.

10. The fight *scene / seen* in the new action film was extremely exciting!

11. Please do not *waist / waste* food from the canteen – take less if you are not hungry.

12. I am a *guessed / guest* at an extremely important event tonight.

13. Please may I have an extremely small *peace / piece* of chocolate cake?

14. The train was *stationary / stationery* on the platform for quite some time.

15. The *sealing / ceiling* on the envelope came loose and everything fell out.

16. Drinking coffee late at *night / knight* can have strange side *affects / effects*.

17. My aunt *made / maid* me some shorts but they were *too / two* long so I had to *alter / altar* them.

18. The *site / sight* of the wreckage was not far from the coast, just beyond the *key / quay*.

Spot spelling mistakes

Underline the spelling mistake in each sentence and then write out the misspelt word with the correct spelling.

1. Mackenzie loved to play tennis, acording to her friend, Jasper.   _____

2. My auntie cooked a delicious vegatable curry when I visited her.   _____

3. I sensably decided to make a plan before beginning my project.   _____

4. Who is definately coming to my party later this month?   _____

5. As well as fireworks, my cats are extremely frightened of lightening.   _____

6. I will be completly ready for the competition next week after this

   last rehearsal.   _____

7. Algebra is basicly learning to problem-solve with numbers and letters.   _____

8. I need to mark on my calender when all my friends' birthdays are so

   that I don't forget them.   _____

Underline the correct spelling of the word that completes each sentence.

9. The library's *reference / refference / referance* section was useful for my project on local history.

10. The house was *hansome / handsome / handsom* and had been well looked after.

11. As she was a very *careful / carful / carefull* chess player, she beat many opponents.

12. Our new puppy (a cute yellow Labrador) is very *exciteable / exiteable / excitable*.

13. The *miserable / misrable / miserible* builder cheered up when the rain stopped.

14. My *neihbour / nieghbour / neighbour* is an extremely good musician.

15. I waved *enthusiasticly / enthusiasticaly / enthusiastically* so my friend would see me in the crowd.

16. Would you like to go to the cinema *tomorow / tomorrow / tommorrow*?

Synonyms and antonyms

Synonyms are words that have the same meaning. For example, **large**, **huge**, **enormous**, **gigantic**, **gargantuan**, **massive** and **immense** all mean 'of sizable proportion'.

Antonyms are words which mean the opposite of one another. For example, **sad**, **sorrowful**, **downcast**, **miserable**, **mournful**, **joyless** and **gloomy** are all antonyms of **happy**.

 TIP Using synonyms in your writing will help to make your writing more interesting and make sure you don't repeat the same word.

Some antonyms can be made by adding a prefix to a word or by changing a suffix.

tidy → **un**tidy   fire → **mis**fire
agree → **dis**agree   hope**ful** → hope**less**

(!) Always check carefully whether you are being asked to find a synonym or an antonym. Do not get them mixed up.

Some questions ask you to identify the synonym or antonym of a given word.

> Underline the word on the right that means the same as the word in bold on the left.
>
> **rubbish**   decline refuse wasteful

This question is asking you to find a synonym of the word 'rubbish'. First, see if there are any words that you know are not the right word. The word 'decline' means 'decrease' or 'say no', so it cannot mean 'rubbish'.

Then look to see if any words are similar, but not the same part of speech. The word 'wasteful' is related to 'rubbish'. However, 'wasteful' is an adjective whereas 'rubbish' is a noun.

The verb 'refuse' (pronounced with a stress on the second syllable) means 'decline' or 'say no' to something, but the noun 'refuse' (pronounced with a stress on the first syllable) has the same meaning as 'rubbish' (meaning waste material). Therefore, 'refuse' is the correct answer.

Answer: rubbish   decline <u>refuse</u> wasteful

 Underline the word on the right that means the same as the word in bold on the left.

1.   **abandon**   ceasefire leave advance

2.   **clash**   conflict agree hit

3.   **accomplish**   fail accept achieve

4.   **diminish**   decrease enlarge detailed

5.   **skilful**   novice competent complicated

6.   **diligent**   slow care hard-working

7.   **perplex**   bewilder confusing unintelligent

8.   **convey**   letter retain carry

Schofield & Sims

Synonyms and antonyms

Here is another example of a question asking you to find the synonym or antonym of a given word.

> Underline the word on the right that is opposite in meaning to the word in bold on the left.
>
> **slack**   trousers loose tight

This time you are being asked to find an antonym – a word that is opposite in meaning.

The word 'slack' sounds similar to the American word 'slacks', meaning trousers, but it does not mean the same thing – you must watch out for similar sounding words.

Sometimes you can look for affixes such as dis–, un– or –less to give you the antonym, but not here.

You must think whether you have heard the word before in a sentence or an idiom. An example might be 'these tent ropes are very slack', meaning they are too loose. Therefore, the word 'slack' means 'loose'. The opposite of 'loose' is 'tight'.

Answer: slack   trousers loose <u>tight</u>

  Always check carefully whether you are being asked to find a synonym or an antonym.

  Underline the word on the right that is opposite in meaning to the word in bold on the left.

9. **total**   partial enough similar

10. **timid**   shy time bold

11. **peaceful**   tranquil agitated floating

12. **courteous**   civil kingly rude

13. **nourish**   malnourished starve nurture

14. **bow**   stern bend stick

15. **trivial**   quizzical odd important

16. **amiable**   friendly hostile generous

 Make sure that you think about all the possible meanings of the words you're given when you're looking for a synonym or an antonym.
For example, the word 'watch' can be a verb (I **watch** the match) and a noun (I wear a **watch**).

Sometimes, you will be given a grid of words to choose from.

Use the grid to answer the question below.

young	spiteful	contemporary
malevolent	unkind	considerate
new	ancient	melancholy

Find **three** synonyms for the word 'cruel'.

Cross off words that mean the opposite of 'cruel', such as 'considerate'. You can also cross off any words you know the meaning of and which are not connected to 'cruel', such as 'young', 'ancient' and 'new'.

Once you have done this, you are left with fewer words ('unkind', 'spiteful', 'contemporary', 'malevolent' and 'melancholy'). Look for the obvious synonyms first. 'Cruel' is the opposite of 'kind'. The suffix un– means 'not', therefore 'unkind' must mean the same as 'cruel'. 'Spiteful' means 'full of spite', which relates to being cruel and is therefore a synonym.

You are left with words you may not know. There are several strategies you can try to work out the answer. Either you can try to think of sentences where you might have heard them before, or you can put them into sentences and see if they sound correct. For example, you might have heard of contemporary music or dance, so 'contemporary' is unlikely to be a synonym for 'cruel'.

You could also think about similar words and their prefixes. The antonym of 'malevolent' is 'benevolent'. The prefix mal– means 'bad' and bene– is a prefix meaning 'good'.

Therefore, 'malevolent' must mean the same as 'cruel'. The word 'melancholy' means 'sad'.

Answer: malevolent, spiteful, unkind

 Use the grid to answer the questions below.

17.

persuade	fortunate	assure
happy	sway	rich
blessed	dissuade	lucky

   i)   Find **three** synonyms for the word 'convince'.

   _____ _____ _____

   ii) Find **three** antonyms for the word 'unfortunate'.

   _____ _____ _____

Synonyms and antonyms

You may be asked to fill in the missing letters in a word to make a synonym.

Add the missing letters to the word on the right to make a synonym of the word on the left.

adore   c h __ r i __ __

First, decide what part of speech the word must be. In this example, 'adore' is a verb so the synonym must also be a verb.

Then think of words you know which contain these letters and are also synonyms of the word 'adore'. If you cannot think of the right synonym, try to think about what letters might fit sensibly in the gaps. For instance, in this example, the next letter after 'ch' is likely to be a vowel.

Answer: ch**er**i**sh**

You may also have to make an antonym. Check carefully to see what the question is asking for.

Add the missing letters to the word on the right to make an antonym of the word on the left.

tiny   e __ __ r m __ u s

As before, think about the word class of the words. Here, 'tiny' is an adjective, so the antonym must also be an adjective. Think of any adjectives that have the opposite meaning to 'tiny' that you can remember and see if they fit with the letters you have been given.

If you cannot think of the word, think about what the missing letters could be. Adjectives often end in –ous, so try that. If the rest of the word doesn't come to mind, work through letters of the alphabet to see what might fit.

Answer: e**no**rm**ous**

 Add the missing letters to the word on the right to make a synonym of the word on the left.

18. abundant   __ l e n __ __ f __ __

19. mix   c o m __ __ __ e

20. realm   k __ __ g d __ __

21. serene   __ e a c __ f u __

22. brave   h e __ __ __ c

23. doze   __ n o __ __ e

Add the missing letters to the word on the right to make an antonym of the word on the left.

24. assemble   d i __ m __ n t __ __

25. chaotic   t r __ __ __ u i __

26. reward   __ u __ i __ __

27. frivolous   s e __ __ __ u s

28. rigid   __ l e __ i __ l e

29. succeed   f __ __ l

Synonyms and antonyms

As part of a comprehension exercise, you may be given a word and asked to find a word in a passage which means the same or the opposite.

Use the passage to answer the questions below.

As the lions relaxed on the grassy plain, they contemplated the day ahead. For some, the day would be full of exciting escapades down at the watering hole. For others, it would mean enduring the sweltering heat of the sun and attempting to find shade under the large, wafting leaves of a tree.

Find a synonym in the passage for the word 'adventures'.

Think about the meaning and word class of 'adventures'. It is a noun and is often accompanied by words such as 'thrilling' or 'fun'. In this case, you can see that the word 'exciting' has been used with the word 'escapades'. If you read ahead, it also mentions a watering hole, which could be a fun place. Therefore, the synonym must be 'escapades'.

Answer: escapades

Find an antonym in the passage for the word 'freezing'.

'Freezing' is an adjective meaning extremely cold or a verb meaning to make something extremely cold. The word meaning the opposite would be describing something that is extremely hot. The sun is mentioned with the adjective 'sweltering'. Therefore, this must mean the opposite of 'freezing' as the sun is extremely hot. The antonym for 'freezing' is therefore 'sweltering'.

Answer: sweltering

 Use the passage to answer the questions below.

Even in the supposedly desolate landscape of the desert, you can be lucky enough to come across abundant wildlife. At certain times of the year, after heavy rainfall, delicate desert flowers burst into bloom. Tiny frogs emerge from their sandy hiding places to enjoy the cool water which collects in large pools, and larger animals come to feed upon the luscious plants which sprout up from the desert floor.

30. Find synonyms in the passage for the following words.

i) barren _____

iii) torrential _____

ii) encounter _____

iv) infinitesimal _____

31. Find antonyms in the passage for the following words.

i) insufficient _____

iii) scarce _____

ii) unfortunate _____

iv) robust _____

 TIP Synonyms and antonyms can sometimes be short phrases rather than single words. Make sure you only copy the essential words in your answer.

Schofield & Sims

Homonyms

A homonym is a word which is spelt the same as another word, but which has a different meaning. For example, the word 'bank' can mean an institution where money is deposited or withdrawn, or it can mean the side of a river or lake.

Homonyms are not to be confused with homophones, which are words that sound the same as each other but which have a different spelling (homophones are covered in more detail on page 55).

Some homonym questions might ask you to choose one word that will complete two different sentences sensibly.

Write **one** homonym to complete both sentences sensibly.

April fed a _____ that was swimming in the pond.

They had to _____ down low as the bird swooped overhead.

First, look at what type of word is needed in each sentence. In the first sentence, the missing word is preceded by the article 'a'. The missing word is probably a noun beginning with a consonant.

Then consider what word would make sense in the context. The clues are 'fed' and 'swimming in the pond'. The answer must be a living creature that is found in ponds. 'Duck', 'fish', 'swan' and 'goose' could all be possibilities. However, the word must also make sense in the second sentence.

The missing word in the second sentence is preceded by the **modal verb** 'had to'. Another verb always follows a modal verb, so the answer must be a verb. Out of the four possible nouns for sentence one, only 'duck' and 'fish' can also be a verb. However, 'fish' doesn't make sense in the second sentence, so the answer must be 'duck', which does.

Answer: duck

Write **one** homonym to complete both sentences sensibly.

1. She could not _____ his crying any longer.

   A huge brown _____ ran out of the cave.

2. He had to be very _____ as he waited for his turn.

   The next _____ in the waiting room was looking very anxious.

3. There were many new _____ starting at school this year.

   His _____ were wide with fright.

4. She couldn't _____ all the attention.

   The _____ on the spade was loose.

5. The spy had to _____ the signal from the enemy.

   Raspberries make a delicious _____ to put on toast.

6. A dark shadow seemed to _____ above him.

   An antique _____ for weaving was exhibited at the museum.

Homonyms

You may also be given two definitions and asked to come up with one word that has both meanings.

> Write the **one** word that has both meanings.
>
> loved and cherished
>
> expensive

In this case, the answer is likely to be an adjective as both the definitions are describing the properties of things. Often, you will be able to guess one of the definitions. 'Dear' is a word that is commonly used to describe something expensive, so it could be the answer.

If you are unsure, you could try putting both words into sentences using the contexts given in the definitions.

I'm visiting a **dear** friend. ⟵——————————— In this context, 'dear' means loved.

The designer sweatshirt was too **dear** for me. ⟵——— Here, 'dear' means expensive.

The word 'dear' makes sense in both of these contexts.

Answer: dear

Write the **one** word that has both meanings.

7. a metal container

   to be able to _____

8. an adverb meaning to move from a higher position to a lower position

   soft, fluffy feathers found on a young bird _____

9. to move your hand back and forth repeatedly

   a regular disturbance in a body of water _____

10. sensitive or painful to the touch

    gentle and loving _____

11. to jump or leap

    the time of year when trees come into blossom _____

12. a small nocturnal animal

    to strike or hit _____

13. distant or inaccessible

    the device used to change channels on a TV _____

14. a journey or excursion

    to fall or stumble _____

Schofield & Sims

Cloze

Cloze is a task where you are asked to fill the gaps in a sentence or passage. You may be given some letters as clues, but more commonly you have to choose words from a list.

Using each of the words in the box below once, complete the paragraph by filling in the missing words.

adolescent	document	fantasy	Witchcraft	series	British	resulting

In the early twenty-first century, a new children's _____ took the world by storm, _____ in a widespread craze for all things wizard. The title? Harry Potter. A series of seven _____ novels written by _____ author J.K. Rowling, the books _____ the exciting and challenging adventures of the _____ wizard Harry Potter from Hogwart's School of _____ and Wizardry.

First, look at the types of words that may fit in the gaps. For instance, an adjective is the most likely word type to come between 'seven' and 'novels'. The obvious choice is 'fantasy' as this is a **genre** of novel. Similarly, 'Witchcraft' has a capital, so must start a sentence or be part of a name or title. The name of the school is included with a gap in the middle and 'Witchcraft' will fit there.

Follow this process throughout. If you are not sure of a word's meaning, leave it until last. If there are still spaces, make a sensible guess based on the word's meaning or word class.

Answer: In the early twenty-first century, a new children's **series** took the world by storm, **resulting** in a widespread craze for all things wizard. The title? Harry Potter. A series of seven **fantasy** novels written by **British** author J.K. Rowling, the books **document** the exciting and challenging adventures of the **adolescent** wizard Harry Potter from Hogwart's School of **Witchcraft** and Wizardry.

Using each of the words in the box below once, complete the paragraph by filling in the missing words.

1.

habitat	kingdom	eyesight	superior	prey	swoop	distinguish

Peregrine falcons are large birds of _____ found on all continents except Antarctica, where the _____ is too hostile. You can easily _____ them from other birds as they have a distinctive greyish-blue back, white underbelly and a black head. They are _____ hunters whose highly developed agility and _____ mean they can prey on other birds and bats in mid-flight. When a peregrine falcon spots its prey, it will _____ down in a dive that can reach up to 200mph. This makes it the fastest in the animal _____.

Abbreviations, acronyms and initialisms

An abbreviation is a shortened form of a word or expression. Abbreviations also include words that are shortened to letters when written but which you still pronounce as the full words, such as etc. (et cetera) and Mr (Mister). They sometimes include a full stop after the last letter to show that they have been abbreviated.

television → telly advertisement → advert
rhinoceros → rhino approximately → approx.

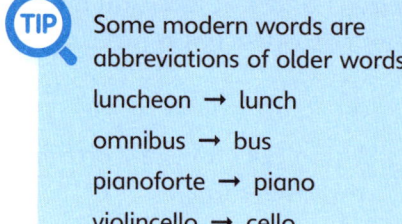

TIP Some modern words are abbreviations of older words:

luncheon → lunch
omnibus → bus
pianoforte → piano
violincello → cello

An acronym is made from the first letters of the words in a name or phrase. It is pronounced as a single word.

President **o**f **t**he **U**nited **S**tates → **POTUS**
Graphic **I**nterchange **F**ormat → **GIF**
Self-**C**ontained **U**nderwater **B**reathing **A**pparatus → **SCUBA**

An initialism is made from the first letters of the words in a name or phrase, but unlike an acronym is pronounced as individual letters.

British **B**roadcasting **C**orporation → **BBC**
Federal **B**ureau of **I**nvestigation → **FBI**
Please **t**urn **o**ver → **PTO**

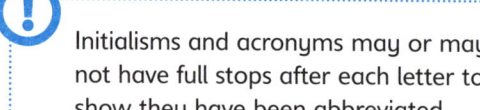 Initialisms and acronyms may or may not have full stops after each letter to show they have been abbreviated.

PTO and P.T.O. are both correct forms.

Make sure you can identify whether words are abbreviations, acronyms or initialisms. It is also useful to know what some common abbreviations, acronyms and initialisms mean.

Identify whether this is an abbreviation, acronym or initialism.

FYI

First, try to say the word. If it is impossible or awkward to say as a single word rather than as individual letters, it is likely to be an initialism. In this case, you say the letters of FYI (for your information) separately, so it is an initialism.

Answer: initialism

Identify whether these are abbreviations, acronyms or initialisms.

1. SWAT _____

3. BLT _____

2. flu _____

4. UNICEF _____

Give the full word or phrase for these abbreviations, acronyms and initialisms.

5. ad _____

7. ASAP _____

6. UK _____

8. app _____

Schofield & Sims

Compound words

Compound words are words containing two or more smaller words that together form a new word with a different meaning.

tea **+** pot = **teapot**   week **+** end = **weekend**

There are several different formats of compound word questions. Often you will be given two groups of words. You must find the two words, one from each group, which go together to form one new compound word. The word from the first group always comes first in the new compound word. Other questions might give you a set of words and ask you to find another word that can go before or after them. Always read the question carefully to see what you are being asked to do.

Underline the **two** words, **one** from each group, that go together to form a new word.

(kick moon butter)   (where light pass)

Try the first word in the group with each word in the second group:

kick **+** where = **kickwhere**   kick **+** light = **kicklight**   kick **+** pass = **kickpass**

To your knowledge, are any of these real words? No. Move on to the second word in the first group. Try it with each word in the second group:

moon **+** where = **moonwhere**   moon **+** light = **moonlight**   moon **+** pass = **moonpass**

Moonlight sounds correct, but just to be sure, keep trying. You may find another word that is more familiar and obvious:

butter **+** where = **butterwhere**   butter **+** light = **butterlight**   butter **+** pass = **butterpass**

None of these are real words. **Moonlight** must be the correct answer.

Answer: (kick <u>moon</u> butter) (where <u>light</u> pass)

 Underline the **two** words, **one** from each group, that go together to form a new word.

1.   (know think like)   (help ledge slip)

2.   (shield dagger spear)   (moss grass mint)

3.   (by me lay)   (wall path pass)

Find **one** word that can be put in front of each of these words to make four new words.

4.   sing   cup   ring   pot   _____

5.   mill   surf   swept   screen   _____

6.   son   front   horse   shell   _____

 The words that make up a compound word may sound very different on their own compared to when they are brought together. For example, **be** and **have** sound very different when they come together to form **behave**.

Now test your skills with these practice pages. If you get stuck, go back to pages 64 to 73 for some reminders.

Synonyms and antonyms

Underline the word on the right that means the same as the word in bold on the left.

1. authentic   simple genuine happy

2. jovial   merry calm good

Underline the word on the right that is opposite in meaning to the word in bold on the left.

3. scarce   rank rare ample

4. surge   stream dwindle diminished

Use the grid to answer the questions below.

5.

fearless	inspire	delayed	obstruct
hinder	extroverted	discourage	upset
dishearten	thwart	shy	unabashed

i)   Find **three** synonyms for the word 'block'.

_____   _____   _____

ii)   Find **three** antonyms for the word 'timid'.

_____   _____   _____

Add the missing letters to the word on the right to make a synonym of the word on the left.

6.   laborious   t __ r e __ __ m __

7.   delay   p __ s __ p __ ne

Add the missing letters to the word on the right to make an antonym of the word on the left.

8.   dull   v __ __ i __

9.   minute   c o __ o __ __ a __

Use the passage to answer the questions below.

The Mole had been working very hard all the morning, spring-cleaning his little home. First with brooms, then with dusters; then on ladders and steps and chairs, with a brush and a pail of whitewash; till he had dust in his throat and eyes, and splashes of whitewash all over his black fur, and an aching back and weary arms. Spring was moving in the air above and in the earth below and around him, penetrating even his dark and lowly little house with its spirit of divine discontent and longing. It was small wonder, then, that he suddenly flung down his brush on the floor, said, "Bother!" and "O blow!" and also "Hang spring-cleaning!" and bolted out of the house without even waiting to put on his coat.

Extract from *The Wind in the Willows* by Kenneth Grahame.

10.   Find synonyms in the passage for the following words.

i)   labouring   _____

ii)   bucket   _____

iii)   piercing   _____

11.   Find antonyms in the passage for the following words.

i)   pleasure   _____

ii)   energetic   _____

iii)   dawdled   _____

Vocabulary practice page 2

Homonyms

Write **one** homonym to complete both sentences sensibly.

1. It was so damp that _____ was growing everywhere.

    I need to _____ the clay to make a vase.

2. She played the _____ so well that everyone got up to dance.

    Do not _____ with the buttons or they will come loose.

3. At _____ time I shall have to finish my homework.

    If you're not careful, you will _____ the seal on that container.

4. The rug was made of cow _____.

    If we are going to do the treasure hunt properly, we must _____ the gold

    deep in the ground.

5. There is so much cream in this sauce that it is too _____ for me.

    She earnt so much money that she was now a _____ woman.

6. In the attic, he found an old, dusty _____ of his favourite rock band.

    The birds sound so beautiful, I must _____ their singing on my phone.

7. I am finally feeling _____ after a bout of the flu.

    We must find a _____ if we are not going to die of thirst in the desert.

Write the **one** word that has both meanings.

8. a small enclosure

    a instrument used for scribing _____

9. went up or increased

    a type of flower with thorns _____

10. a large box with a hinged lid

    the part of the person's body that the arms and legs are attached to _____

11. to break down food in the body

    to understand and assimilate information _____

12. a sum of money given out as a penalty

    very thin or narrow (as in thread) _____

Cloze

Using each of the words in the box below once, complete the paragraph by filling in the missing words.

1.

species	lizard	extending	mobile
ability	continent	grip	surroundings

Chameleons are a beautiful type of _____ that are mostly found on the

_____ of Africa. There are over 150 different _____.

Many of these have the _____ to change colour, which helps them to

increase or decrease their temperature, to communicate with other chameleons or to blend in

with their _____.

Chameleons have some distinctive physical features. In particular, their toes – two of which face

forward and two of which face backward – assist their _____ and agility.

They also have long, thin, _____ tongues and eyes that are independently

_____ to give them a wide view of their surroundings.

Using each of the words in the box below once, complete the paragraph by filling in the missing words.

2.

intelligences	globe	affairs	scrutinised
believed	century	complacency	multiply

No one would have _____ in the last years of the nineteenth

_____ that this world was being watched keenly and closely by

_____ greater than man's and yet as mortal as his own; that as men

busied themselves about their various concerns they were _____

and studied, perhaps almost as narrowly as a man with a microscope might scrutinise

the transient creatures that swarm and _____ in a drop of water.

With infinite _____ men went to and fro over this

_____ about their little _____, serene in

their assurance of their empire over matter.

Extract from *The War of the Worlds* by H.G. Wells.

Abbreviations, acronyms and initialisms

Identify whether these are abbreviations, acronyms or initialisms.

1. U.F.O. _____
2. F.A.Q. _____
3. NIMBY _____

4. vs. _____
5. NASA _____
6. Rd. _____

Give the full word or phrase for these abbreviations, acronyms and initialisms.

7. DIY _____
8. phone _____
9. PIN _____

10. E.T.A. _____
11. AWOL _____
12. lunch _____

Compound words

Underline the **two** words, **one** from each group, that go together to form a new word.

13. (sun sky wind)   (flight shine dark)

14. (before during after)   (night noon morning)

15. (help leader male)   (ship full lace)

16. (life live love)   (hood boat mate)

17. (mouth arm tooth)   (save board pick)

18. (eye ear toe)   (net bat ball)

19. (man sit will)   (age now tone)

20. (near all hang)   (on by met)

Find **one** word that can be put in front of each of these words to make four new words.

21. come   at   have   am   _____

22. tally   night   wed   day   _____

23. not   teen   did   dies   _____

24. draw   hold   stand   in   _____

25. self   on   ring   ding   _____

26. pad   hole   word   board   _____

Identifying text types

Texts can be categorised as either fiction or non-fiction. Within each category, there are many different sub-groups or genres. You can identify a genre by its key features and conventions. Texts can belong to more than one genre, but there is usually one genre that they share most features of.

Fiction texts

Fiction is a style of writing in which the writer uses their imagination to make up stories, characters and events. Usually, they use **prose** – continuous writing made up of full sentences and divided into paragraphs. Fiction texts usually have a clear beginning, middle and end, feature characters and often include sections of dialogue, action and description.

 Fiction texts can be inspired by real events, such as World War II, or real characters, such as Henry VIII. The writer uses their imagination to write a story based on the past.

These are some of the most common genres of fiction.

Realistic fiction is set in a believable setting and contains events that could actually happen in real life. Realistic fiction can be comical or serious. Examples are *Wonder* and *The Boy in the Dress*.

Historical fiction is set in the past and is often based on a real historical event or period. It often includes lots of descriptive detail to help the reader build up a picture of that time in history. Examples are *Street Child* and *War Horse*.

Fantasy fiction is usually set in an imagined place and includes elements that are impossible, such as talking animals or magical powers. Examples are *The Hobbit* and *The Lion, the Witch and the Wardrobe*. **Science fiction** is a type of fantasy fiction that includes science and technology and is often set in space, in another world or in the future. Examples include *A Wrinkle in Time* and *The Hitchhiker's Guide to the Galaxy*.

Adventure fiction contains exciting situations involving action, risk and danger as part of the main plot. Often, adventure stories include a journey or voyage or take place in a faraway land. Examples include *Treasure Island* and *Journey to the River Sea*.

Mystery fiction usually consists of a suspenseful story about a puzzling event, such as a theft or a murder, that is not solved until the end of the story. Authors of mystery fiction often use plot twists to build up suspense and keep the reader guessing. Examples are *Emil and the Detectives* and *The Curious Incident of the Dog in the Night-Time*.

Horror fiction often contains monsters, ghosts and other characters whose purpose is to scare the reader. It may be set in spooky places, such as graveyards or haunted houses. Authors of horror fiction often use tension to create a frightening atmosphere. Examples are *Dracula* and *Beast Quest*.

Myths are a type of traditional tale. They are often sacred stories, set in the past or in another part of the world. They often feature gods or heroic characters and often set out to describe how the world came into being. Examples include 'Pandora's Box' and 'Tiddalick'.

Legends are stories from the past that embellish and exaggerate the life of a real person. The story makes them famous for their deeds. Examples include stories about King Arthur and Robin Hood.

Fairy tales are traditional stories written for children that feature magical and enchanted forces. They usually have a 'happily ever after' ending, where good is rewarded and evil is punished. Examples are 'Cinderella' and 'Beauty and the Beast'.

Fables are very short stories that indirectly teach the reader a moral lesson. In many fables, the characters are animals. Examples are 'The Hare and the Tortoise' and 'The Boy who Cried Wolf'.

Folk tales are short stories that are typically passed on through the generations by word of mouth. Examples include 'The Pied Piper of Hamelin' and 'Mulan'.

Schofield & Sims

Identifying text types

Other texts are not written in prose but are still fiction.

Poetry explores one idea or thought in a series of lines which may not be complete sentences. Poems are usually broken up into **verses** (also known as stanzas), where each verse describes a different aspect of the main idea. Poets often express their thoughts and feelings in a poem. Poems may have a distinctive **rhythm** and can have a **rhyme scheme**. Poets often use different techniques such as **metaphors**, **alliteration** and **onomatopoeia** (see pages 88 to 91) to convey meaning. Examples include 'Isn't my name magical?' and 'I Wandered Lonely as a Cloud'.

In **film scripts** or **play scripts**, the writing is divided into scenes and made up solely of dialogue and stage directions. The plot is revealed only in this way. Examples include *Macbeth* and *Harry Potter and the Cursed Child*.

Make sure that you are able to identify the genre of a text based on its features and conventions.

Identify which genre of fiction the following passage is from.

He <u>froze</u> on the spot and then <u>turned slowly</u>, wondering who – or what – was breathing so heavily down his neck. His <u>eyes gaped open</u> as <u>the hideous creature</u> stared <u>ferociously</u> at him, <u>blood dripping</u> from its <u>fangs</u>.

Underline key words from the text which give clues about the genre and decide which genre most of its features come from. The underlined words suggest that the character is being threatened by a monster. It is a frightening image, and the author appears to be building suspense. Although it could be from several genres (for example, fantasy, adventure), the best fit would be the horror fiction genre.

Answer: horror fiction

 Identify which genre of fiction the following passages are from.

1. The storm was building in strength and ferocity. They clung on to the sides of the little boat with all their might. Pain surged through Jenna's body and she feared she might not be able to hold on for much longer. Would they all survive the night? _____

2. Alfred shivered in the corner. The soot from the chimney had avalanched down the stack and covered the floor. He knew his master would be very angry. Perhaps he'd be sent back to the workhouse! _____

3. Megan waved her wand furiously, but nothing happened. She was starting to panic. Somehow, she had to change Minky back into a cat before the others noticed. _____

4. Long ago, there lived a lonely prince in a castle high on a hill. He longed for a family but had been cursed by an evil wizard whose spell meant he could never set foot beyond the castle's high walls. _____

Identifying text types

Non-fiction texts

Non-fiction texts are based on facts or are texts about real people, things and events. Many non-fiction text types have special structures or formats that can help you to identify them. However, make sure you can identify each type of text even when these features are not used.

There are many different types of non-fiction texts.

Autobiographies and **biographies** are true accounts of real people's lives, either written by themselves (autobiographies) or by someone else (biographies).

 Remember that the prefix auto– means 'self', so someone writing an 'autobiography' is writing about themselves.

Newspaper and **magazine articles** may be recounts or reports about real people, places or events, or articles offering advice or an opinion. They often have an eye-catching headline and are written in columns.

Letters and **emails** are written correspondence from one person to another to give information, express a point of view, address an issue or recount an event. They may be written in formal or informal language.

Diaries are first-hand recounts of a person's personal thoughts about the day in general or a specific event. They often start with a phrase like 'Dear diary'.

Instructions are commands given in a particular order for people to follow, such as a recipe or instructions for building a piece of furniture. These are often (but not always) organised using bullet points or a numbered list.

Information or **reference texts** give information or explanations about specific topics, such as in an encyclopedia.

Leaflets and **brochures** are often intended to persuade the reader to buy something, give information about a range of services on offer or give advice. **Posters** and **flyers** are brief forms of writing to give clear and concise details about a product, service or other important piece of news or information. All of these can be used to create **advertisements**. They can be written to persuade or inform.

Travel writing is a recount or description from the writer's point of view of a journey or experience in another geographical location.

Speeches are texts that are intended to be spoken aloud to an audience. Lots of speeches are written to persuade audiences. The speaker often speaks directly to the audience and uses techniques like short sentences and **rhetorical questions** to make the speech dramatic and keep the audience interested in what they are saying.

Reviews are texts that express an opinion about something that the writer has experienced. This could be a book they have read, a film they have watched, a place they have visited, or an item they have bought. The purpose of the text is to give the reader information that will help them decide whether to choose the experience or not. The review provides a summary of the experience including its positive and negative aspects and includes the writer's own opinion about it.

A blog is a piece of writing found on a website. It is usually a series of entries written about a theme. It often gives a writer's own personal perspective on a topic and may include their own experience or research. The style is often informal and chatty. Topics may include, lifestyle and fitness, music, travel, sports, technology or fashion.

Identifying text types

You need to be able to identify the genre of a non-fiction text.

Identify which genre of non-fiction the following passage is from.

I am deeply concerned to hear that you were unhappy with your experience at my restaurant. I do hope that I can put forward some proposals of how to compensate you for your distress.

Underline key words from the text which give clues as to which genre the text may be from. Then look at the list and decide which is the most appropriate genre that the underlined words fit into.

<u>I am deeply concerned</u> to hear that <u>you were unhappy</u> with your experience at my restaurant.

I do hope that I can put forward some proposals of <u>how to compensate you</u> for your distress.

The underlined words suggest that someone is writing to another person. It is part of a greater correspondence. Therefore, it must be written correspondence – either a letter or an email.

Answer: letter or email

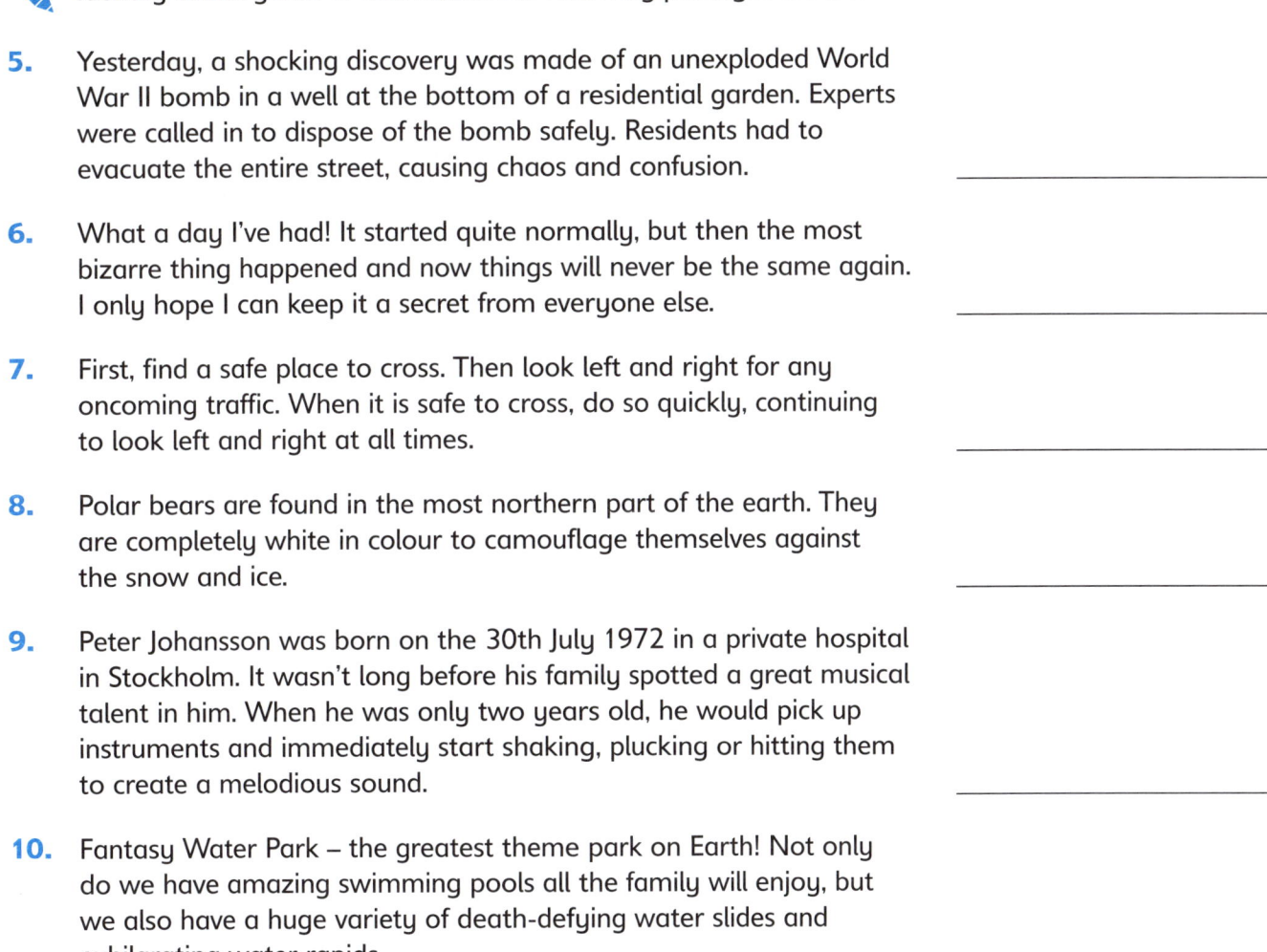 Identify which genre of non-fiction the following passages are from.

5. Yesterday, a shocking discovery was made of an unexploded World War II bomb in a well at the bottom of a residential garden. Experts were called in to dispose of the bomb safely. Residents had to evacuate the entire street, causing chaos and confusion.

_____

6. What a day I've had! It started quite normally, but then the most bizarre thing happened and now things will never be the same again. I only hope I can keep it a secret from everyone else.

_____

7. First, find a safe place to cross. Then look left and right for any oncoming traffic. When it is safe to cross, do so quickly, continuing to look left and right at all times.

_____

8. Polar bears are found in the most northern part of the earth. They are completely white in colour to camouflage themselves against the snow and ice.

_____

9. Peter Johansson was born on the 30th July 1972 in a private hospital in Stockholm. It wasn't long before his family spotted a great musical talent in him. When he was only two years old, he would pick up instruments and immediately start shaking, plucking or hitting them to create a melodious sound.

_____

10. Fantasy Water Park – the greatest theme park on Earth! Not only do we have amazing swimming pools all the family will enjoy, but we also have a huge variety of death-defying water slides and exhilarating water rapids.

_____

Retrieving information from texts

Finding information in a text quickly and accurately is an important skill in comprehension. It requires you to **skim** and scan the text efficiently.

Skimming a text

When you skim a text, you allow your eyes to float across it, only looking for the most important points and key words that give you a general idea of what the writing is about. When you first encounter a text, it is a good idea to skim it and underline the main points and key words.

TIP Key words are things that tell you **who**, **what**, **why**, **when**, **where** and **how**.

Look at the example below. The main points and key words are underlined.

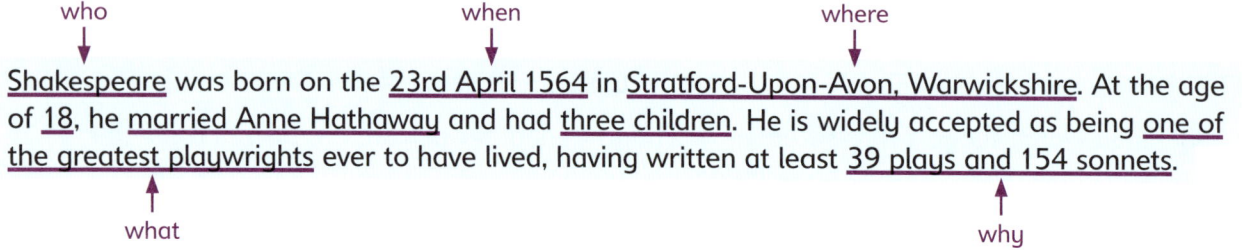

who ↓   when ↓   where ↓

Shakespeare was born on the 23rd April 1564 in Stratford-Upon-Avon, Warwickshire. At the age of 18, he married Anne Hathaway and had three children. He is widely accepted as being one of the greatest playwrights ever to have lived, having written at least 39 plays and 154 sonnets.

↑ what   ↑ why

Scanning a text

When you scan a text, you allow your eyes to look for specific words that will lead you to the precise information you need to answer a **who**, **what**, **why**, **when**, **where** or **how** question.

> The Tasmanian devil is what's known as a carnivorous marsupial. Thanks largely to its depiction in a popular cartoon, it's the most well-known of this small group of animals. It has also been the largest carnivorous marsupial since the extinction of the Tasmanian tiger in 1936. Although it is also endangered, it can still be found in the wild on Tasmania, an island off the south-east coast of Australia.
>
> What event made the Tasmanian devil the largest carnivorous marsupial in the world?

First, underline the key words in the question.

What event made the Tasmanian devil the largest carnivorous marsupial in the world?

Now you can look for these words in the text and they should lead to the answer. The word 'event' does not appear in the text, but the event described in the text will be your answer. When you have found the answer, underline it.

The Tasmanian devil is what's known as a carnivorous marsupial. Thanks largely to its depiction in a popular cartoon, it's the most well-known of this small group of animals. It has also been the largest carnivorous marsupial since the extinction of the Tasmanian tiger in 1936. Although it is also endangered, it can still be found in the wild on Tasmania, an island off the south-east coast of Australia.

Answer: The extinction of the Tasmanian tiger made the Tasmanian devil the largest carnivorous marsupial in the world.

Retrieving information from texts

 Skim the passage below and underline the main points and key words.

1.   Martin Luther King Jr was born in Atlanta, USA on 15th January 1929. In the 1950s, he became

a leading activist and spokesperson in the civil rights movement, which protested against racial

discrimination in the southern American states. As a Baptist minister, he promoted non-violent

protests, including marches and acts of civil disobedience. This approach was partly inspired by

the work of Mahatma Gandhi in India, but also reflected his own religious beliefs.

 Read the passages and answer the questions that follow. Remember to use skimming and scanning to help you.

2.   The Tasmanian devil looks a bit like a large rat. However, Tasmanian devils have larger, more muscular bodies and distinctive dark fur. These animals have a surprisingly strong voice and can make a mixture of sounds from snorts to disturbing screeches. It is easy to see how they earnt their reputation for getting enraged, especially when they are feeding, when they can become ferocious. They also have one of the most powerful bites of any surviving land mammal due to their large head and mighty jaws.

   i)   What is particularly disturbing about a Tasmanian devil?

   ii)   What is evident when a Tasmanian devil feeds?

   iii) What makes the Tasmanian devil have such a powerful bite?

3.   Fareeda was tired of walking. She had been traipsing through the forest since dawn but was still lost. She wished she hadn't noticed the woodpeckers feeding and wandered off; that way, she would have kept up with her brother, Omar, who was marching at such a pace only an army soldier could've matched his speed. They were running away from their village, having escaped a huge fire that was sure to burn everything in its way. How did it start? Only Omar knew.

"Are you there?" she called in vain. She had tried countless times to call for help but no one answered. She looked around with unease – was she safe? Was anyone following her? Only the scuttling of the squirrels and hedgehogs could be heard. Dark clouds were looming overhead. The sun was lowering in the sky and the temperature had dropped. She had to find shelter soon.

   i)   Where is Fareeda?

   ii)   Why is Fareeda tired?

   iii) Why did Fareeda and her brother need to escape the village?

   iv)   Which **three** animals does Fareeda see or hear in the woods?

   v)   Why does Fareeda need to find shelter soon?

Using inference and deduction

In comprehension, you will often need to read between the lines to **infer** meaning or to **deduce** information from clues given in the text. Writers don't always make things obvious – sometimes, information may be implied or not directly stated. You must be a detective and seek out the clues that give you the information you need.

Mrs Jones swung open the classroom door and stormed into the room.

"Who has stolen my memory stick with all the answers to the exam questions on it?" she barked. Everyone shuddered. Nobody dared move for fear of her reaction.

How is Mrs Jones feeling?

There are a number of clues in the text to tell us how Mrs Jones feels.

She opened the door violently.   The word 'stormed' suggests aggression.

Mrs Jones <u>swung open the classroom door</u> and <u>stormed</u> into the room.

The word 'barked' calls to mind an angry, possibly frightening, dog.

"Who has stolen my memory stick with all the answers to the exam questions on it?" she <u>barked</u>.

The children are scared.   She is angry and they are scared of what she may do.

Everyone <u>shuddered</u>. Nobody dared move for <u>fear of her reaction</u>.

In this passage, Mrs Jones is clearly angry, even though the writer doesn't explicitly say this.

Answer: Mrs Jones is feeling angry.

"There you go," the man behind the desk said, handing Jason the pile of books. "That'll keep you busy for a while."
"Not for long," Mum said, smiling. "I'm sure we'll be returning these by next week."

What is the man's job?

Start by underlining his actions, which may offer some clues.

The man is serving Jason and Mum. He works with books. He could be a bookseller or librarian.

"There you go," <u>the man behind the desk</u> said, handing Jason <u>the pile of books</u>. "That'll keep you busy for a while."

She's talking about returning books even though she's happy, so the man is probably a librarian.

Mum is happy with his service.

"Not for long," Mum said, <u>smiling</u>. "I'm sure we'll be <u>returning these by next week</u>."

You can deduce from these clues that the man is a librarian.

Answer: The man is a librarian.

 TIP To infer means to give an interpretation that goes beyond the literal information given in the text. To deduce means to come to a conclusion based on evidence in the text.

Schofield & Sims

Read the passages and answer the questions that follow.

1. The sun hung low and heavy in the sky, no brighter than a dying ember. Trees spun with white lace stood frozen, as if in a deep and peaceful slumber. As far as the eye could see, a blanket of white was draped over hills and fields, and, dotted here and there, thin ribbons of smoke curled upwards into the sky.

   Down by the lake, Nadia and Lottie chattered as they finished tying their skates. Lottie's skates fitted well, but Nadia, who had borrowed her friend's old pair, had needed to wear three pairs of thick socks to make them fit.

   "Ready?" asked Lottie, pushing back the woollen hat that kept falling over her eyes and grinning.

   Heart fluttering like a hummingbird, Nadia hesitated for a moment, then nodded. "Ready."

   i) What time of year is the passage set in?

   _____

   ii) What are the two girls about to do? Where are they going to do it?

   _____

   iii) Who do you think is more experienced at this activity? Use evidence from the text to explain your answer.

   _____

   _____

   iv) How is Lottie feeling in the passage? Use evidence from the text to explain your answer.

   _____

   v) How is Nadia feeling in the passage? Use evidence from the text to explain your answer.

   _____

   _____

   _____

2. When people saw Fawn Sprocket scuttling down the road, they crossed to the other side to avoid her judging eyes. There was no 'Good morning' if you were unlucky enough to dodge past her – only a sniff and a grunt as if she were admonishing you for your audacity to share the pavement with her.

   What kind of person was Fawn Sprocket? Use evidence from the text to explain your answer.

   _____

   _____

   _____

Identifying word meanings

Some questions require you to decipher the meaning of less familiar words as they are used in texts. Sometimes you might be given possible meanings to choose from, but at other times you might have to use the context to work out the meaning of an unfamiliar word.

Having a wide vocabulary will be useful here. There are also several different strategies you can use.

1. Look for clues in the rest of the sentence.

There was a huge array of **beverages** such as milkshakes, smoothies and juices to choose from.

Here the list of examples in the second half of the sentence gives you a clue about the meaning of the word 'beverages'. Milkshakes, smoothies and juices are all types of drinks, so the word 'beverages' must mean **drinks**.

2. Use your knowledge of word classes.

He was completely **morose** – a frown spread across his face like a dark cloud and he grumbled about the state of the weather.

In this sentence, you can tell that 'morose' must be an adjective as it is describing a man. You can then look for other clues in the sentence that show what the man is doing. It says that he is frowning and grumbling. These are signs that somebody is upset. Therefore, 'morose' must mean **sad**, **moody** or **grumpy**.

 TIP When you have decided what the word means, you could try putting your new word back into the sentence to check that the meaning of the sentence hasn't changed and that the word class matches. This works best when your meaning is only one or two words, like the example here.

3. Look for an explanation elsewhere in the text.

In many courts in Europe, a **troubadour** was a very important part of palace life. Whenever the king or queen required entertainment, he would perform his songs and poetry to the delight of the royal family and courtiers.

Here, the first sentence only says that 'troubadours' were an important part of palace life. You must look further on in the text to find out what a troubadour is.

The second sentence says that a 'troubadour' was an entertainer who 'would perform his songs and poetry'. This suggests that he wrote all his compositions. Therefore, a 'troubadour' is a **performer**, **entertainer** and **composer of music and poetry**.

4. Look for words that are similar, or use your knowledge of spelling rules.

The **polyphonic** nature of the performance was mesmerising.

Your knowledge of common prefixes and suffixes can be very useful when answering questions about word meanings. You may know that the prefix poly– means 'many' and that –phonic means 'sound'. Therefore, the word 'polyphonic' must mean **that the performance contains many sounds**, probably voices or instruments.

 TIP Take a look back at pages 51 to 52 for a reminder about the meanings of some common prefixes and suffixes.

Schofield & Sims

Explain the meaning of the word 'reproached' as it is used in this sentence.

Miss Lucas reproached Samuel for borrowing Cole's favourite pen without asking first.

In this sentence, the clues are 'borrowing' and 'without asking first'. Samuel should have asked before he borrowed someone's property. You could guess that Miss Lucas, who is probably his teacher, might be telling him off or reminding him of the rules. You can also tell that the word is a verb as it ends in –ed and comes straight after the subject. Therefore, 'reproached' must mean 'told off'.

Answer: told off

 Always use the context of the sentence to work out the meaning of the word. Some words have more than one meaning – it is important to find the meaning that fits the sentence in front of you.

Explain the meaning of the word 'fretful' as it is used in this sentence.

My mum always worries about whether I am eating healthy food, but if she were a little less fretful, she'd be a lot more fun.

Here, the writer says that their mum would be 'more fun' if she was 'less fretful'. This suggests that 'fretful' has a meaning that is opposite to fun. If you read the sentence again, you see that it says that their mum 'always worries'. The word 'fretful' has the suffix –ful, meaning 'full of', which is similar to 'always'. If 'fretful' meant 'full of worries', it would have a meaning that was the opposite of fun.

Answer: full of worries

 Explain the meaning of each underlined word as it is used in the sentence.

1. The mansion, with its splendid ballroom and decadent banqueting suite, was decidedly <u>palatial</u>. _____

2. It can be difficult to forgive someone who has hurt you, even if that person is <u>penitent</u> and expresses regret for their actions. _____

3. My brother wanted to get the red balloons for the party and my sister wanted to get the green balloons, but I'm not concerned about such <u>frivolous</u> things. _____

4. I won the game with a lucky roll, but Sarah had the <u>audacity</u> to suggest that I had cheated. _____

5. The <u>laborious</u> nature of fruit picking meant that not many people applied for the job. _____

6. The spy in the film <u>furtively</u> gathered confidential information from a number of sources and then returned home. _____

 TIP Some comprehension questions will ask you to identify word types (for example, verbs, adjectives, prepositions or adverbs) in a text. Have a look back at pages 9 to 25 to remind yourself about how to tackle these questions and look out for questions of this type in the Comprehension practice pages.

Literary techniques

It is important that you are familiar with the wide range of techniques that are used to make writing more interesting and memorable.

The most important techniques are known as figurative language or imagery. They are choices of words or phrases which create a strong image in your mind. Often the words and phrases are not used literally but have an alternative meaning.

Here are some important techniques to know and be able to identify. You can also use them in your own writing.

Similes compare something with the qualities of something else using the words 'like' or 'as'.

Her hair was **like** rats' tails. ◄——— Rats' tails are long, straggly and quite probably dirty. By using this comparison, the writer is suggesting that her hair is tangled and messy.

It was **as** cold **as** the North Pole. ◄——— The North Pole sounds like the coldest place on Earth. By using this comparison, the writer is emphasising that it couldn't get any colder.

Metaphors are a stronger comparison. You are saying that something **actually is** something else. The reader knows that this is not literally true, but it helps them build a more vivid picture in their mind, meaning that it is easier to imagine the thing being described.

The tennis player **was** a grumbling volcano, and he exploded when he lost.

Volcanoes are often associated with anger and this one sounds like it is about to erupt, so describing a tennis player as one suggests he is getting more and more angry as the game goes on.

Like similes, **analogies** use comparison to create a description. However, there are some differences between the two literary techniques. An analogy compares one thing with another in order to explain one of its features or qualities. The two things analogies compare can often be very different, so they often need to be longer than similes to explain how the two things are similar. They encourage the reader to think about and reflect on the ideas they suggest.

Life and roller coasters are two completely different things.

Life **is like** a roller coaster. **Both have** their ups and downs.

It is only when you focus on the fact that both have 'ups and downs' that you realise what is similar about them.

Personification is when human attributes are given to something non-human. These attributes could be anything from physical characteristics to human behaviours and emotions. The human attributes can be given to something physical, like an animal or an object, or they can be given to something abstract, like an emotion.

Giving the tree 'fingers' suggests that its branches are bare, long, thin and twisted.

The tree's **gnarled fingers grasped at** the sky.

The words 'grasped at' suggest that the branches are stretching towards the sky on purpose. These elements of personification together make the tree seem eerie and otherworldly.

Excitement **raced** through the crowd as the runners approached the finish line.

In reality, 'excitement' is an emotion – it cannot do anything by itself. Here, the author has made it act like a human to show that the whole crowd is excited about the outcome of the race.

Schofield & Sims

Literary techniques

Other techniques are connected more with the sounds of words. When you notice them in texts, think about the effect they have on your reading.

Alliteration is when two or more words begin with the same sound. Any sound can be used for alliteration and it can be repeated any number of times.

the **h**elpless **h**owling of the **h**apless **h**ound

 Alliteration is repetition of the same letter sound, rather than just of the same letter. **P**ink **ph**one does not contain alliteration as the 'p's do not make the same sound (one makes a 'p' sound and one a 'ff' sound).

By repeating the 'h' sound, the writer is emphasising the desperate plight of the hound. The reader is more likely to remember this image thanks to the repeated sound.

 TIP There can be 'little' words around words that start with the same sound to create alliteration. For example, The **W**ind in the **W**illows.

Assonance is the repetition of vowel sounds in a series of words.

Sh**e** tried to cr**ee**p past the sl**ee**ping sh**ee**p.

The repetition of the long 'ee' sound creates a soft, slow sound, mirroring the movement the girl is trying to make to avoid waking the sheep.

Sibilance is the name for a special type of alliteration. It is the name used when there are a lot of soft consonant sounds (mainly 's' and 'sh'). These sounds can be found anywhere in the word.

The **s**oft, **s**ilky **s**and bru**sh**ed up again**s**t the **s**mooth gra**ss**.

The repetition of the 's' and 'sh' sounds creates a calming effect.

 TIP If you can't remember the names for these literary techniques in the exam, don't worry. You can describe what the author has done and say what effect it has on the reader instead. For example:

The author uses lots of 's' and 'sh' sounds to make the landscape seem calm and peaceful.

Onomatopoeia is when words sound like the noises they are describing.

The steam train **screeched** into the station.

The 'ee' sound in 'screeched' is a bit like the sound a steam train would make when its brakes were applied. The sound effects are used to create a sound in your head that is memorable and adds to the picture being created in your mind.

Repetition is when a word or phrase is repeated to emphasise a point. It can be used to change the pace and create atmosphere.

The wind blew through the trees; **the wind blew** across the field; **the wind blew** around the houses.

Repeating the phrase 'the wind blew' emphasises the strength and range of the wind. It makes you imagine the weather when you picture the setting, making it more realistic.

On this page and the next are some other techniques to look out for.

An **oxymoron** is a figure of speech containing words that seem to contradict one another.

> The burst of **friendly fire** was unexpected.

This is a military term. It relates to an injury caused by the guns of an ally. However, fire is never friendly and usually causes harm.

> The **silence** was **deafening**.

This is also an oxymoron – silence does not make any noise, so it cannot be deafening. This oxymoron is used to mean that someone is uncomfortable with the silence or lack of response.

A **euphemism** is a mild word or expression that is substituted for one considered to be too harsh or impolite when referring to something unpleasant.

> He is **between jobs** at present.

This is a polite way of saying he is unemployed. It avoids using a word that has negative associations.

Proverbs are short, well-known expressions of popular wisdom.

> **An apple a day keeps the doctor away.**

This proverb tells us that eating fruit will keep us healthy. It is memorable so more likely to be followed.

An **idiom** is a phrase that has a different meaning to the usual meaning of the words. Idioms are usually used in more informal writing.

 TIP Both proverbs and idioms use well-known phrases, but they do not do the same thing. Idioms describe things in creative ways. Proverbs offer advice. Make sure you can remember the difference.

> He looked **down in the mouth**.

This means that he is sad. By saying 'down in the mouth', it is suggesting he is not smiling, his mouth is turned down in a frown and therefore that he is sad. It is a strong image that is easy to remember.

 TIP A list of common idioms can be found on the Schofield & Sims website.

A **cliché** is an overused phrase. Writers often let characters use these and try to think of their own original descriptions for their main narratives.

> He ran around **like a headless chicken**.

This is also a simile, but it is often used to describe someone behaving in an out-of-control manner. It is better to use clichés sparingly.

Rhetorical questions are questions where the answer is so obvious you don't need to answer it. They are often included in persuasive writing with a personal pronoun, such as 'you', to engage the reader.

> **Wouldn't it be wonderful to jet off to a tropical island for your next holiday?**

Obviously, it would! This is an effective technique because you are likely to read on to find out how this is possible.

Literary techniques

Irony is a technique where the opposite thing happens to what the reader expects, or something is said which is the opposite of what they mean. It is memorable as there is a twist in what is said. Irony is often used to create humour.

It has been reported that the fire station has burnt down.

This is ironic as it would be the last place you would expect a fire – where firefighters are stationed!

"Well, she was as friendly as a rattlesnake!"

This is ironic because it means the opposite – a rattlesnake is clearly not friendly.

Sarcasm is a less polite, more unkind form of verbal irony.

"Nice perfume – must you marinate in it?"

This means the speaker thinks the perfume smells too strong – it's not a nice smell at all.

You may be asked to identify different literary techniques being used in texts.

Which technique is this an example of?

He was smiling like a Cheshire cat.

As it contains the word 'like' this is a simile. It is comparing the person's smile to that of the Cheshire cat, which is large and wide.

Answer: simile

(!) Sometimes, sentences can contain more than one literary technique. For example, 'The wind whooshed through the wicked witch's window' contains alliteration as well as onomatopoeia. Look out for examples of this in the practice questions.

 Identify the literary techniques that are used in each of these sentences.

1.   Gosh, it's raining cats and dogs out there!   _____

2.   His legs were jelly and his heart was a beating drum.   _____

3.   Red sky at night, shepherd's delight.   _____

4.   The weeping willows waved drowsily in the weak westerly wind. _____

5.   The car coughed and spluttered as it started.   _____

6.   I must go and spend a penny.   _____

7.   Our only choice was to keep going.   _____

8.   How funny – the traffic warden just got a parking ticket!   _____

9.   How many times have I asked you not to call out in class?   _____

10. The racing car zoomed around the track.   _____

Comprehension question types

Depending on the exam you are taking, you may have to answer comprehension questions in multiple-choice format, where you are given several possible answers to choose from. Alternatively, you may get standard format questions, where you have to write your answers in full sentences.

When approaching either type of question, there are two key things you should do first:

1. Read the question very carefully. It might help to underline key words that you will need to look out for in the text.

2. Read the text carefully. You could also underline key words or phrases as you go. This keeps you reading actively, taking in all necessary information.

Multiple-choice questions normally don't have a number of marks indicated on the test. You only need to follow the instructions and pick the correct answer.

Still the Ghost pointed downward to the grave by which it stood.

"Men's courses will foreshadow certain ends, to which, if persevered in, they must lead," said Scrooge. "But if the courses be departed from, the ends will change. Say it is thus with what you show me!"

The Spirit was immovable as ever.

Scrooge crept towards it, trembling as he went; and following the finger, read upon the stone of the neglected grave his own name, EBENEZER SCROOGE.

Extract from *A Christmas Carol* by Charles Dickens.

Whose name did Scrooge see on the gravestone?

A. The Ghost's name

B. His father's name

C. His name

D. Another man's name

For this question, you need to look out for key nouns and verbs.

Whose name did Scrooge see on the gravestone?

You can assume the whole passage is about the character, so there is no need to underline his name.

Now scan the text for the key words 'name' and 'gravestone'. Think about the fact that gravestones might also be referred to as 'stones' or 'graves', so treat these words as key words too. In the last line, you will notice that several of the key words appear together:

Scrooge crept towards it, trembling as he went; and following the finger, read upon the stone of the neglected grave his own name, EBENEZER SCROOGE.

Read around the key words to find the right answer. The text says it is 'his own name' and you can double check that the name it is referring to is the one that the question is asking you to find. It is, so the answer must be C.

Answer: C

Schofield & Sims

Comprehension question types

In standard format questions, if questions are worth 1 or 2 marks you can give simple answers made up of one or two sentences. However, if the questions are worth more marks you may need to give your answers in more depth.

> The door of Scrooge's counting-house was open that he might keep his eye upon his clerk, who in a dismal little cell beyond, a sort of tank, was copying letters. Scrooge had a very small fire, but the clerk's fire was so very much smaller that it looked like one coal.
>
> Extract from **A Christmas Carol** by Charles Dickens.
>
> How is Scrooge portrayed in this passage? Use evidence from the text to explain your answer.
>
> /6

The key word in this question is 'portrayed', which means you need to describe how he is represented or depicted. Underline anything that gives clues about Scrooge's behaviour or opinions.

The door of Scrooge's counting-house was open that <u>he might keep his eye upon his clerk</u>, who in a <u>dismal little cell</u> beyond, a sort of tank, was copying letters. Scrooge had a <u>very small fire</u>, but the <u>clerk's fire was so very much smaller</u> that it looked like one coal.

The underlined clues show that Scrooge is miserly and unkind to his employee. Since the question asks for evidence, include these quotes in your answer.

Answer: The text tells us that Scrooge leaves his door open so that he 'might keep his eye upon his clerk', suggesting that he isn't trusting. He keeps his clerk in a 'dismal little cell' and they both have very small fires. This suggests that Scrooge doesn't like to spend money and doesn't mind making himself or other people uncomfortable.

 Read the passage and answer the questions that follow.

> The cold became intense. In the main street, at the corner of the court, some labourers were repairing the gas-pipes, and had lighted a great fire in a brazier, round which a party of ragged men and boys were gathered: warming their hands and winking their eyes before the blaze in rapture. The water-plug being left in solitude, its overflowings sullenly congealed, and turned
> 5 to misanthropic ice. The brightness of the shops where holly sprigs and berries crackled in the lamp heat of the windows, made pale faces ruddy as they passed. Poulterers' and grocers' trades became a splendid joke: a glorious pageant, with which it was next to impossible to believe that such dull principles as bargain and sale had anything to do. The Lord Mayor, in the stronghold of the mighty Mansion House, gave orders to his fifty cooks and butlers to keep Christmas as a
> 10 Lord Mayor's household should; and even the little tailor, whom he had fined five shillings on the previous Monday for being drunk and bloodthirsty in the streets, stirred up to-morrow's pudding in his garret, while his lean wife and the baby sallied out to buy the beef.
>
> Extract from **A Christmas Carol** by Charles Dickens.

1. Why had the workers lit a fire?

    A. They wanted to cook some food.   **C.** They were outside and it was cold.

    B. The gas pipes had broken.   **D.** People wanted a party.

2. What was the atmosphere like on the street? Use evidence from the text to explain your answer.

    /6

Now test your skills with these practice pages. If you get stuck, go back to pages 78 to 93 for some reminders.

Read the passage and answer the questions that follow.

A gloomy breakfast was eaten, and the four remaining dogs were harnessed to the sled. The day was a repetition of the days that had gone before. The men toiled without speech across the face of the frozen world. The silence was unbroken save by the cries of their pursuers, that, unseen, hung upon their rear. With the coming of night in the mid-afternoon, the cries sounded closer as
5 the pursuers drew in according to their custom; and the dogs grew excited and frightened, and were guilty of panics that tangled the traces and further depressed the two men.

"There, that'll fix you fool critters," Bill said with satisfaction that night, standing erect at completion of his task. About the neck of each dog he had fastened a leather thong. To this, and so close to the neck that the dog could not get his teeth to it, he had tied a stout stick four or five
10 feet in length. The other end of the stick, in turn, was made fast to a stake in the ground by means of a leather thong. The dog was unable to gnaw through the leather at his own end of the stick. The stick prevented him from getting at the leather that fastened the other end.

Henry nodded his head approvingly.

"It's the only contraption that'll ever hold One Ear," he said. "He can gnaw through leather as
15 clean as a knife an' jes' about half as quick. They all'll be here in the mornin' hunky-dory."

"You jes' bet they will," Bill affirmed. "If one of 'em turns up missin', I'll go without my coffee."

"They jes' know we ain't loaded to kill," Henry remarked at bed-time, indicating the gleaming circle that hemmed them in. "If we could put a couple of shots into 'em, they'd be more respectful. They come closer every night. Get the firelight out of your eyes an' look hard – there! Did you see
20 that one?"

For some time the two men amused themselves with watching the movement of vague forms on the edge of the firelight. By looking closely and steadily at where a pair of eyes burned in the darkness, the form of the animal would slowly take shape. They could even see these forms move at times.

25 A sound among the dogs attracted the men's attention. One Ear was uttering quick, eager whines, lunging at the length of his stick towards the darkness, and desisting now and again in order to make frantic attacks on the stick with his teeth.

"Look at that, Bill," Henry whispered.

Full into the firelight, with a stealthy, sidelong movement, glided a doglike animal. It moved with
30 commingled mistrust and daring, cautiously observing the men, its attention fixed on the dogs. One Ear strained the full length of the stick toward the intruder and whined with eagerness.

"That fool One Ear don't seem scairt much," Bill said in a low tone.

"It's a she-wolf," Henry whispered back, "an' that accounts for Fatty an' Frog. She's the decoy for the pack. She draws out the dog an' then all the rest pitches in an' eats 'm up."

35 The fire crackled. A log fell apart with a loud spluttering noise. At the sound of it the strange animal leaped back into the darkness.

"Henry, I'm a-thinkin'," Bill announced.

"Thinkin' what?"

"I'm a-thinkin' that was the one I lambasted with the club."

Extract from **White Fang** by Jack London.

1. Read the first paragraph. Why do you think night is described as *coming ... in the mid-afternoon*?

    _____   /1

2. What does the word *toiled* mean in line 2?

    _____   /1

3. Which word in line 7 means the same as 'upright'?

    _____   /1

4. Which dog was the most difficult to control? Use evidence from the text to explain your answer.

    _____

    _____

    _____   /3

5. Read from *They jes' know ...* to *... move at times*. Do you think the two men are afraid of the wolves? Use evidence from the text to explain your answer.

    _____

    _____

    _____   /3

6. Find **one** example of onomatopoeia in the text between lines 33 and 38. What effect does it create?

    _____

    _____   /3

7. What is Henry's explanation for the she-wolf's presence? Explain what this means.

    _____

    _____

    _____   /3

8. *One Ear strained the full length of the stick toward the intruder and whined with eagerness.* Give **one** example of each of the following word types from this sentence.

    i)   proper noun _____   iii) verb _____

    ii) abstract noun _____   iv) adjective _____

    /4

Read the passage and answer the questions that follow.

As she was not at all a timid child and always did what she wanted to do, Mary went to the green door and turned the handle. She hoped the door would not open because she wanted to be sure she had found the mysterious garden – but it did open quite easily and she walked through it and found herself in an orchard. There were walls all round it also and trees trained against them, and

5   there were bare fruit-trees growing in the winter-browned grass – but there was no green door to be seen anywhere. Mary looked for it, and yet when she had entered the upper end of the garden she had noticed that the wall did not seem to end with the orchard but to extend beyond it as if it enclosed a place at the other side. She could see the tops of trees above the wall, and when she stood still she saw a bird with a bright red breast sitting on the topmost branch of one of them,

10   and suddenly he burst into his winter song – almost as if he had caught sight of her and was calling to her.

She stopped and listened to him and somehow his cheerful, friendly little whistle gave her a pleased feeling – even a disagreeable little girl may be lonely, and the big closed house and big bare moor and big bare gardens had made this one feel as if there was no one left in the world but

15   herself. If she had been an affectionate child, who had been used to being loved, she would have broken her heart, but even though she was "Mistress Mary Quite Contrary" she was desolate, and the bright-breasted little bird brought a look into her sour little face which was almost a smile. She listened to him until he flew away. She liked him and wondered if she should ever see him again. Perhaps he lived in the mysterious garden and knew all about it.

20   Perhaps it was because she had nothing whatever to do that she thought so much of the deserted garden. She was curious about it and wanted to see what it was like. Why had Mr Archibald Craven buried the key? If he had liked his wife so much why did he hate her garden?

Extract from **The Secret Garden** by Frances Hodgson Burnett.

1. Read from the beginning of the text to ... *found herself in an orchard.* What impression do you get of Mary? Explain your answer using evidence from the text.

_____

_____   /3

2. Why did Mary hope that the green door wouldn't open?

_____   /1

3. What is an *orchard*?

_____   /1

4. What does the word *sour* mean in line 17?

_____   /1

5. Read the last paragraph. How does the author make the garden sound mysterious? Give **one** way and explain your answer.

_____

_____

_____   /3

Read the passage and answer the questions that follow.

Pierre Toussaint was born a slave. He vowed that when he was free, he would do all he could to help those who suffered.

Until the age of 21, Pierre was kept on a plantation on the island of Haiti with his sister Rosalie. As slaves in the household of the Bérard family, they were treated better than many others:
5 Pierre was taught to read and write, and to speak English and French. But they were not free to leave. When the people of Haiti began to rebel against slavery, the Bérards left for New York City, USA, taking Pierre and Rosalie with them. New York was very different to the islands of the Caribbean, with new laws and opportunities. Pierre was able to work outside of the family home as a hairdresser, and when his owners died, he was set free. He had earned enough money to buy
10 Rosalie's freedom too.

Pierre then devoted his life to helping the poor of New York City. He paid for the freedom of another slave, Juliette Noel, who became his wife. The couple adopted Rosalie's daughter after Rosalie died of tuberculosis and soon after, the Toussaints opened up their home to other orphans and began fostering abandoned children. Pierre also arranged financial aid for refugees and,
15 because of his language skills, helped many French-speaking immigrants to find jobs. When New York suffered an outbreak of the deadly disease cholera, Pierre repeatedly risked his own life to visit quarantine houses to nurse the sick.

Despite being a respected businessman, Pierre still encountered racist attitudes from people who believed that those born as slaves should always remain slaves. Even though he donated money
20 towards the building of a new cathedral in the city, he was refused entry to it when it first opened because of the colour of his skin.

When Pierre died in 1853, he was buried in the cemetery of the cathedral. For many years he was forgotten, but in the twentieth century his extraordinary kindness was recognised and began to be celebrated. In 1996, Pope John Paul II declared Pierre 'venerable'.

Extract from ***The Good Guys: 50 Heroes Who Changed the World with Kindness* by Rob Kemp**, reproduced by permission of Hodder Children's Books.

1.   Where was Toussaint until the age of 21?

   A.   in a metal processing plant with his siblings

   B.   on a plantation with his sister

   C.   in a factory in Jamaica

   D.   on a farm in Haiti

2.   Why was Toussaint better off than most slaves?

   A.   He was fed well.

   B.   He was given free time.

   C.   He was given a basic education.

   D.   He was allowed to have a pet.

3.   How did his circumstances change when he moved to New York?

   A.   He could vote.

   B.   He could work in a different establishment.

   C.   He could get his hair cut.

   D.   He could become a gardener.

4. What unfortunate incident befell Rosalie?

   A. She died of a terrible illness.

   B. She lost her job.

   C. She became homeless.

   D. She died in childbirth.

5. Which two words in the text refer to people coming from abroad?

   A. tourists and visitors

   B. refugees and immigrants

   C. French-speaking and teacher

   D. slaves and immigrants

6. How did Toussaint risk his life?

   A. by taking up a dangerous sport

   B. through violent protests

   C. by caring for people with dangerous diseases

   D. through challenging the opposition

7. What cause did he make a generous donation towards?

   A. the building of a museum

   B. the building of a monastery

   C. the building of an abbey

   D. the building of a cathedral

8. Who recognised Toussaint's importance many years later?

   A. the president of the United States of America

   B. Pope John the first

   C. Pope Paul the second

   D. Pope John Paul the second

9. What is the purpose of this text?

   A. to give an opinion about what Toussaint was like

   B. to tell a story about something that happened to Toussaint

   C. to give a general account of Toussaint's life with lessons to inspire

   D. to persuade us to become doctors

10. What does the word *venerable* mean in line 24?

    A. made famous

    B. thought to be magical and saint-like

    C. thought to be poisonous

    D. accorded a great deal of respect

Schofield & Sims

Read the poem and answer the questions that follow.

The moon has a face like the clock in the hall;
She shines on thieves on the garden wall,
On streets and fields and harbour quays,
4 And birdies asleep in the forks of the trees.

The squalling cat and the squeaking mouse,
The howling dog by the door of the house,
The bat that lies in bed at noon,
8 All love to be out by the light of the moon.

But all of the things that belong to the day
Cuddle to sleep to be out of her way;
And flowers and children close their eyes
12 Till up in the morning the sun shall arise.

'The Moon' by Robert Louis Stevenson.

1. What literary technique does the poet use in line 1? Give its name and describe why it is effective.

_____

_____ /3

2. What is the meaning of *forks* in line 4?

_____ /1

3. What contrast is made between the cat and the mouse?

_____

_____ /2

4. Find **one** example of personification in the poem. Why has it been used?

_____

_____ /3

5. What is the general atmosphere in the poem? Use evidence from the text to explain your answer.

_____

_____ /3

6. Describe the rhyme scheme of the poem. What effect does it create?

_____

_____

_____ /3

The writing task

As part of your exam, you may be expected to write a piece of creative writing for between 30 and 60 minutes.

It is not possible to predict exactly what kind of writing task you will get – it is different in every exam.

However, some examples of the sorts of writing tasks you might get in the exam are listed below.

- You may be given a title, such as 'Lost', 'Storm at Sea' or 'The Uninvited Guest', as inspiration for a piece of **narrative writing**. Most titles will lend themselves to a problem that has to be resolved in some way. Alternatively, a title may lend itself to a piece of **descriptive writing** – for example, 'The Busy Train Station', 'A Park in Spring' or 'Someone I Admire'.

 Make sure you know the difference between narrative writing (see pages 102 to 104) and descriptive writing (see pages 105 to 106).

- You may be given a sentence or short extract from a story to read and then be asked to continue it in your own words.

- You may be given a picture to base a story or description on. It may be a picture of a scene or of characters.

- You may be given a headline (for example, 'New Species Discovered' or 'Gorilla Escapes from Zoo!') and be asked to write a newspaper report.

- You may be asked to write a persuasive letter or speech. For example, you may be asked to write to your local council to demand that the local leisure centre is not closed; write a speech encouraging people to vote for you to become the school newspaper editor; or write a letter to your parents asking for an exotic pet.

- You may be given a fiction extract to read and then be asked to write something from the perspective of one of the characters. For example, you could be asked to read a passage about an explorer. Once you have done that, you might have to write a letter as if you are that explorer writing to a family member to explain your adventures so far. Another example may be a diary entry that you are asked to write as a character based on an event that has taken place in an extract.

- You may be asked to write about a personal experience you have had, such as a frightening event, a time when you did something you regret or a favourite birthday.

- You may be given some facts and asked to relate them in a piece of informative or persuasive writing. For example, you may be given some information about head lice that you must write into an advisory leaflet designed to reassure children and parents about how to tackle them.

- You may be asked to read a poem or extract and then write an essay about how the writer uses effective techniques to present the characters or situation.

- You may be given a topic or question and asked to write an essay giving your personal opinion on it. For example, should mobile phones be banned from schools?

This is not an exhaustive list. You must be prepared for anything!

 TIP If you are familiar with the different types of fiction and non-fiction texts, you will find it easier to answer different types of writing task. You can review the text types on pages 78 to 80 to see some of the main text types and their typical features.

Schofield & Sims

The writing task

Below is a list of the key things you should think about when you are completing any writing task. If you follow these guidelines, you should be able to approach any task confidently.

It is also a good idea to practise writing a range of different types of texts, develop banks of interesting words and phrases you can draw upon in the exam, and create skeletons for essays and stories which you can adapt and apply to a range of questions on the day. However, also be prepared to think quickly on the day to generate a new idea if necessary.

There are several things you should think about when writing.

TIP Reading different text types will help improve your writing because you will become more familiar with a range of different features.

- Your structure should link well to the task and have a clear introduction, middle and conclusion. Paragraphs should be developed and detailed. A good planning strategy will help ensure that your writing has a good structure. See pages 110 to 113 for explanations on how to plan narrative, descriptive and non-fiction writing.

- You should include a good range of language techniques including effective choices of vocabulary that take into account the specific features normally found in the type of text you are writing, such as persuasive techniques, description and figurative language. For explanations of how to use figurative language in your work, see page 115. You must also think about whether your writing requires a formal or informal tone and consider what person your writing should be in. Look back at pages 78 to 80 for the features of different text types.

- Your writing should have a good range of sentence structure and variation. This includes using simple, compound and complex sentences, and imperatives, questions and exclamations as well as statements. There should also be a range of sentence openers and sentence lengths to show control and intentional effects. See pages 117 to 118 for varying sentence structure.

- Your language should be accurate and demonstrate a strong knowledge of spelling, punctuation and grammar to a sophisticated level. The grammar, spelling, punctuation and vocabulary sections of this book will support your learning in this area.

Narrative perspective

Writing can be written in the first, second or third person.

In the first person, the writer writes about themselves using pronouns like **I**, **me**, **we** and **us**.

In the second person, the writer writes directly to the reader using pronouns like **you** and **your**.

In the third person, the writer is writing about other people and characters using pronouns like **he**, **she** and **they**.

You must think about which person you need to use for your writing task. For example, a diary is normally written in the first person, persuasive writing often makes use of the second person and a descriptive piece tends to be written in the third person.

The rest of this section will provide a step-by-step approach to tackling different text types in the writing task. At each stage, there will be opportunities to practise the techniques covered. The practice pages at the end of the section provide lists of writing tasks for you to attempt once you understand the process.

Features of narrative writing

Narratives are stories containing a plot that builds in tension and excitement towards a final conclusion. You may be given a title or the first sentence, or you may be expected to continue the story from a first paragraph written by someone else.

Beginning

All narratives, even if continuing from a first sentence or paragraph, should start with an introduction setting the scene for the part of the story you are starting or continuing from.

Example one

Write a story with 'The Storm' as the title.

When you are given a title for narrative writing, you need to think about how the title is going to link to your story. You might link it to the beginning, or the beginning might provide a contrast with the title so that the climax is more dramatic later on. This answer provides a contrast.

Answer: "What a lovely day for a fishing trip," I said as we arrived at the dock. We had booked a day trip out on the 'Belle of the Seas' – an old fishing boat from the nineteenth century. I couldn't wait: I'd been looking forward to this since we arrived in Cornwall for our summer holidays.

 TIP Make sure that the atmosphere you create fits well with the prompt. For example, the title 'The Storm' could be about a storm. However, it also suggests danger, so you would want to include conflict in your story.

Example two

Read the sentence and then continue the story.

Despite apparently being alone, he knew someone was there.

When you are given a sentence to continue from, you need to think about what clues are included in that sentence. For example:

The main character is male.

Despite apparently being alone, he knew someone was there.

The main character is alone.

Someone else is around, but it is not clear whether the main character knows them.

You need to link your beginning to the sentence by using the same clues in your writing and then adding more information. This answer gives the male character a name and explains why he is alone.

Answer: Despite apparently being alone, he knew someone was there. Lee had been playing hide and seek in the woods near his house. When no-one came to find him, he decided to head back home.

"Typical Marcus," he grumbled of his friend, "always leaving me." It was getting dark and he had lost his bearings. He looked around uncomfortably. Surely Marcus was long gone by now, probably tucking into the burgers and chips Dad had promised them both for dinner. Yet he didn't feel alone ... Someone was there. He could hear breathing and the crunching of autumnal leaves.

Schofield & Sims

Features of narrative writing

Example three

Read the passage and then continue the story.

Hour after hour passed away, and slowly Dorothy got over her fright; but she felt quite lonely, and the wind shrieked so loudly all about her that she nearly became deaf. At first she had wondered if she would be dashed to pieces when the house fell again; but as the hours passed and nothing terrible happened, she stopped worrying and resolved to wait calmly and see what the future would bring. At last she crawled over the swaying floor to her bed and lay down upon it; and Toto followed and lay down beside her.

In spite of the swaying house and the wailing of the wind, Dorothy soon closed her eyes and fell fast asleep.

Extract from *The Wonderful Wizard of Oz* by L. Frank Baum.

When asked to continue a paragraph, it is a good idea to annotate the paragraph for clues to see how to carry on in the same style.

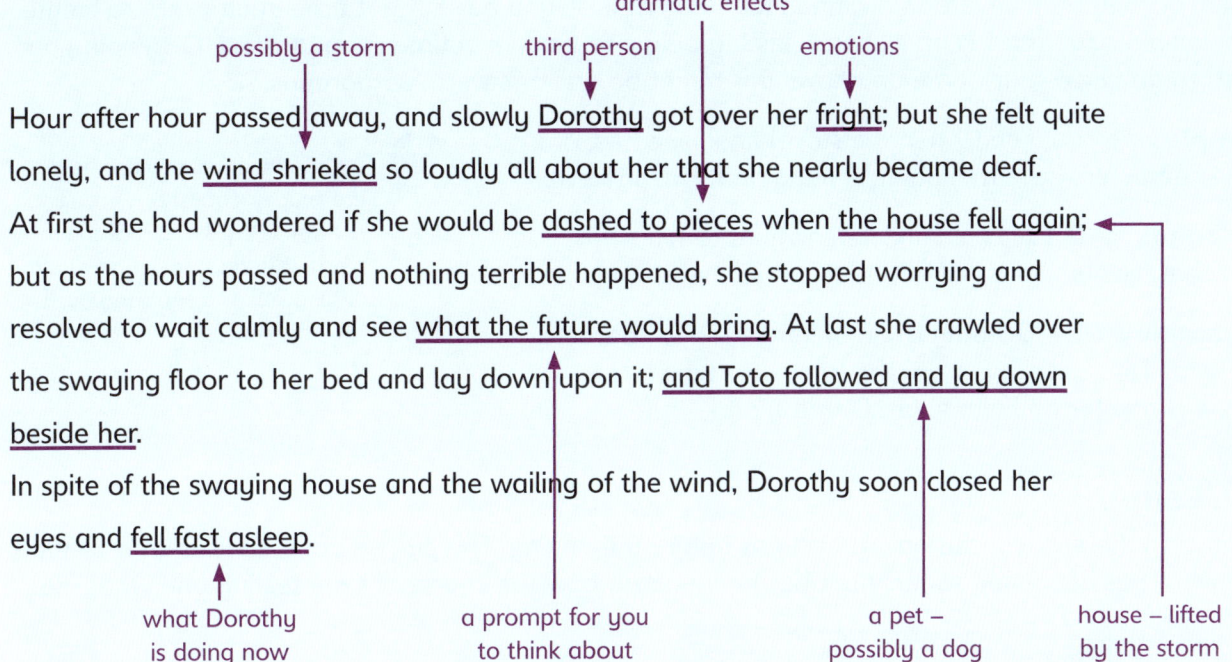

Answer: It must have been hours later when she awoke and she couldn't believe what she saw – all the trees from her garden had been uprooted as if a giant had pulled them out with his bare hands and hurled them into the air, watching them land haphazardly. The door to the house was hanging and creaking from its hinges. But where was Toto? She called, but he was nowhere to be seen. She had to find him.

 Even if you recognise the prompt text from your own reading, you don't need to write about what actually happens. Imagine what could happen based on just the evidence in the passage in front of you and write your own narrative.

Features of narrative writing

Build up and climax

From there, add more and more detail until you reach the high point of the narrative – a climax of tension and excitement. The high point is usually a problem (such as an accident), but in some cases it is the opposite – a happy high point (such as a wedding or an amazing discovery). You will need to develop the build up and climax over several paragraphs.

In **Example one**, the high point could be the storm at full strength and descriptions of how the characters cope with it. Perhaps the boat struggles because it is so old.

In **Example two**, perhaps it could be the frantic pursuit of someone chasing the main character as he tries to escape.

> (!) Don't spend too long on your build up and climax sections – you must make sure that you have time to write your resolution and conclusion too.

In **Example three**, the high point could be the revelation that Toto is stuck high up in a tree having gone up to explore the devastation that the storm had brought.

Resolution

From there, you must control the story to bring it to an end. This could mean that all the events are resolved, or they may be left on a cliffhanger. Remember – you haven't got time in an exam to create a complex plot. You must keep it simple, lasting only a few hours in time span at most. Depending on your story and how much time you have, this might be one or several paragraphs.

Example one could end when the storm finally ceases, and all the characters have managed to hang on for dear life.

In **Example two**, Lee could find somewhere to hide, but know that his pursuer is still out there somewhere.

> A cliffhanger ending is when all the reader's questions aren't answered by the end of the story. Instead, the action is left unresolved in a shocking or exciting way.

In **Example three**, Dorothy could meet a strange character who helps Toto get down from the tree – but who is the strange character and where are Dorothy and Toto?

Conclusion

This leads to the final conclusion – reflections before the ending. The purpose of a conclusion is to think about what has happened so far, what has been learnt, how the characters are feeling and what may happen next.

Here are some possible conclusions for examples one, two and three.

Example one: I couldn't believe how differently the day had ended compared to my expectations. How had we escaped the jaws of that terrible storm?

Example two: Lee tried holding his breath. He was safe now, but for how long? Where was this other person? He tried to think of reasons why he might be being followed. He'd have to wait until morning. There was no way he could find help in the dark.

Example three: Dorothy held Toto safely in her arms. She was so grateful to this strange little man for his help. But who was he? She had thought she was in her own garden, but now she was not so sure.

Schofield & Sims

Features of descriptive writing

A description is a way of painting a picture of a scene or a person in the reader's mind using words, phrases and descriptive techniques. Unlike narrative writing, descriptive writing does not need a plot. Nothing exciting or dramatic needs to happen. Instead, you just need to show your reader what a place, person or event is normally like. The interesting thing for the reader is how you choose to describe it.

Effective descriptive writing includes many rich sensory details which appeal to the reader's senses of sight, hearing, touch, smell and taste, when appropriate. Descriptive writing may also paint pictures of the feelings of the person, place or thing evoked by the writer.

You can describe smells.

You can describe sounds.

The comforting **aroma of candy floss** wafted through the air as the **excited screams of children** echoed around the amusement park.

You can describe sights.

You can describe tastes.

Shoppers **milled around the makeshift wooden huts, mouths full of sweet hot chocolate**. Many eager hands, **well-insulated with soft woollen mittens**, clutched happily at disposable cups and **the scorching brown liquid burnt many tongues**.

You can describe touch through temperatures.

You can describe touch through textures.

High-quality descriptive writing often makes use of figurative language such as personification, similes and metaphors to help create a clearer picture in the reader's mind.

The fire **sat** in the grate, **chewing up coals** and **spitting out sparks** on to the threadbare carpet.

 TIP Take a look back at pages 88 to 91 for a reminder of the different types of figurative language you can include in your writing.

Effective descriptive writing also uses precise language. Some words, like 'good', 'said' and 'thing', are used all the time. Replace these sorts of general adjectives, verbs and nouns with specific adjectives, verbs and nouns to create a more specific picture in the reader's mind.

Now you know where the mountains are and what they look like.

The **mountains** were **amazing**. → The **snow-capped mountains** were **magnificent, towering over the valley**.

Now you know exactly how the lava was moving.

Lava **was coming** down the road. → **Fiery, blazing** lava **gushed** down the road **like a waterfall**.

Now you know what the house looks like and can make some guesses about what its owner is like.

The **house** had a **garden**. → The **tumbledown cottage covered in moss** sat in **a wild garden, overrun by weeds**.

TIP Look at page 115 for advice on improving your writing with powerful words.

Features of descriptive writing

High-quality descriptive writing is organised. Some ways to organise descriptive writing include: chronologically (time), spatially (location) and in order of importance. When describing a person, you might begin with a physical description, followed by how that person thinks, feels and acts. When describing a setting, you might choose three or four features of the scene to describe in turn.

A good description is like a telescope.

1. The introduction provides a general outline of the atmosphere and an overview of the scene or character. Your introduction will normally be one paragraph, but your paragraph can be as long or short as it needs to be to provide a good overview.

    Dawn in the desert. The temperature is still bearable. Small creatures are scuttling over the sand, trying to find the last few morsels of food.

    She was a formidable person, my mother. Once an opera singer, she was now a smaller, quieter version of herself, looking after my father.

2. Three to four detailed paragraphs then focus in on smaller details, like a telescope zooming in on specific images. Here are some examples of some details that you might include in one of your paragraphs.

    Scuttling across the sand, a scorpion hunts for food before retreating into a hole to escape the heat of the emerging sun. His tiny, beaded body, as shiny as a conker, glistens in the light. Quivering intently, his sting is a constant reminder of his readiness to attack.

    She spent a lot of time these days doing chores: she was endlessly folding bedclothes, washing dishes and heating soup. Yet I noticed, as I carried the washing to help her hang the clothes on the line, that she had never lost her habit of singing her old songs – little snatches of French, Italian and German – under her breath as she worked.

    As you can see from these examples, the key is to find small details and extend them. Try to write at least two or three sentences about each element of the aspect you focus on before moving on to something else. Think of different perspectives too – could you be a vulture looking at and describing the desert? How would that change your description? Perhaps you swoop down to get a closer look …

3. A conclusion then provides a shift in time or atmosphere. The 'telescope' is zooming back out but seeing a change in the overall picture. Again, this will be one paragraph, but how long it is will depend on the time you have for the task and how much you still have to say. Make sure you have time to write at least a short conclusion paragraph.

    As the sun finally drops in the sky, the desert creatures can surface once again from their cool hideouts. Darkness reveals a magical array of sparkling diamonds crowding the sky.

    Although she never said a word, I know that part of her still dreamt of being up on that stage at the Royal Opera House again as she had been in her youth.

 TIP Just like with narrative and non-fiction writing, it is important to plan your descriptive writing before you begin. See page 111 for help with planning descriptive writing.

Features of non-fiction writing

Whatever the genre of non-fiction writing, it must contain a strong introduction setting the scene, three to four detailed paragraphs in the middle developing the key ideas of the piece and a reflective conclusion, summarising the key details and outlining future events or hopes.

In addition, there are certain key structural features for each genre that you need to be aware of.

Structure

Letters

Look at the way the addresses are set out in an informal and formal letter.

23 Pie Street
London
SM4 2LL

1st January 2021

Dear Granny,

[Contents of letter]

Lots of love,

Jennifer

23 Pie Street
London
SM4 2LL

1st January 2021

The Right Honourable Boris Johnson MP
10 Downing Street
London
SW1A 2AA

Dear Prime Minister,

[Contents of letter]

Yours sincerely,

Jennifer Smith

 TIP Write 'Yours sincerely' if you know the name of the recipient of the letter and 'Yours faithfully' if you do not.

Newspaper reports

You may not be asked to set out a newspaper report in the traditional manner, in columns. However, it should still have a strong, catchy headline at the top to intrigue the reader. Often language techniques, such as alliteration or a pun (a play on words), may be used to achieve this. For example, 'Scientists flap with delight at new bird species'.

 TIP Headlines often miss out determiners and other small words. For example, a headline may be 'Rare sheep stolen from farm' rather than 'Some rare sheep have been stolen from a farm'.

Diary entries

Just like a letter, you write the date at the top of the page. You then begin 'Dear diary' as though you are writing to the diary. Unlike a letter, you do not need to put an address or write your name at the end.

Features of non-fiction writing

Beginning

All non-fiction writing must then have a strong introduction, setting the scene. Here are some examples.

Letters

I am writing to you as it has come to my attention that more and more pupils do not know how to cook. I think this is detrimental to our health and well-being. It is certainly not preparing us for our future. I am imploring you to find time in the school timetable to introduce regular lessons in cooking skills for all age groups.

Speeches

I am here today to urge you to consider supporting my charity, The Rainforest Trust. Every day in the newspaper we read heart-breaking stories of poor, defenceless orangutans losing their homes, or of villages being washed away through flooding caused by deforestation. In the last twenty years, more than two-thirds of the world's rainforests have been chopped down mercilessly to make way for the logging industry. This cannot continue. By supporting my charity, you will be changing lives for the better. Here is how.

Diary entries

Dear diary,

Today was a day I shall never forget! I have been searching for my treasure for weeks, months, possibly even years. Today was the day that I finally struck gold! Well, figuratively at least: my treasure was not quite the sort of thing you'd find piled up in a dragon's cave ...

Newspaper reports

Last week, excited scientists announced an extraordinary new discovery in Papua New Guinea when they found a new species of bird. They are calling it the discovery of the twenty-first century. Initially looking to monitor the bird-of-paradise population, scientists soon realised they had found more than they were looking for!

Middle

Your middle paragraphs should then develop each point you are trying to make. Both a diary entry and a newspaper report continue like recounts, retelling events in chronological order, but should still contain dramatic and descriptive language as well as emotions and reactions. You may also wish to include quotes and eyewitness accounts in newspaper reports, to add authenticity and make the report more believable.

Newspaper reports

The scientists had travelled to Papua New Guinea on a fact-finding mission to learn more about the feeding rituals of the bird-of-paradise. However, it wasn't long before they were intrigued to hear not the mellifluous call of the bird they were following, but a much louder, deeper tone which sounded more like a squawk than a tweet.

Schofield & Sims

However, when giving your opinion or trying to persuade the reader of something, the middle paragraphs need a 'topic statement' to begin with, followed by examples and further details to reinforce your points. A 'topic statement' is a summary sentence at the start of a paragraph that tells the reader what the paragraph is going to be about.

Letters

This topic sentence shows the reader that this paragraph is arguing that cooking lessons improve maths skills.

Firstly, cooking lessons provide good opportunities to apply important maths skills. For example, it is important to be accurate when using scales to measure out ingredients. A cake could turn into a culinary disaster if the right measures and ratios are not used.

It is still important to add dramatic and emotive language as well – look at the phrase 'culinary disaster'. This creates a lasting impression in your head. See pages 115 to 118 for help with this.

Facts and statistics are also a good way to back up your point and create the impression that many people support your view.

Speeches

Many people know that the amount of CO_2 in the atmosphere has risen drastically to critical levels over the last twenty years. Within another twenty years, three-quarters of the ice-caps could melt leaving the Arctic wildlife in deadly situations.

Ending

The ending for each non-fiction genre should be reflective but also look to the future. It must conclude the passage decisively.

Letters

I hope that my reasons have convinced you that regular cookery lessons are vital to develop pupils' mathematical skills, life skills and sense of responsibility. It is your ultimate duty to ensure that your pupils are ready for the outside world and challenges of adult life. Please consider my ideas carefully and discuss them further with your staff. I hope that in the near future we will see cookery lessons as a regular part of our exciting and innovative curriculum.

Newspaper reports

Scientists are now continuing their research in other areas of Papua New Guinea in the hope that they may discover more new bird species. They will continue to monitor the population of all birds in the hope of finding out more exciting facts about feeding and breeding.

Diary entries

All in all, it was a very exciting day. The authorities were very grateful that I had alerted them as soon as I'd uncovered the first pieces of pottery and iron. Can you believe that there's going to be a whole archaeological excavation now to see whether there was an ancient settlement nearby? I might even get to help out! For now, though, I had better wash off all this mud and head to bed.

Planning narrative writing

Whether you are continuing a story from a prompt or writing your own story from scratch, the first thing to do is brainstorm lots of ideas. This should take between two and five minutes.

Write a story – real or imagined – about a frightening encounter with an animal.

Create a simple mind map of your ideas. Then choose your favourite to develop into a plan. Do not include too many events or have your narrative take place over too long a period of time. Developing just one or two details well is better than a long list of underdeveloped events.

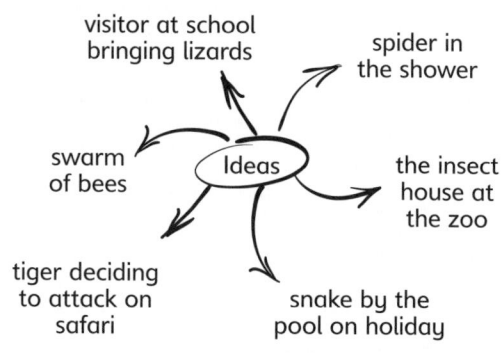

Now you are ready to create your plan. Plot the climax – the most tense part of your story – on to it first. Your plan can be a story mountain or simply a list of bullet points.

With the pivotal point of your story now in the middle, you can balance out the rest of the story – the beginning, build up, resolution and conclusion. Remember – the story doesn't have to be completely resolved at the end; you could finish it with a cliffhanger. However, it still needs a conclusion that shows there is more to come. If it is a continuation of the story, you still need to set the scene for the next part.

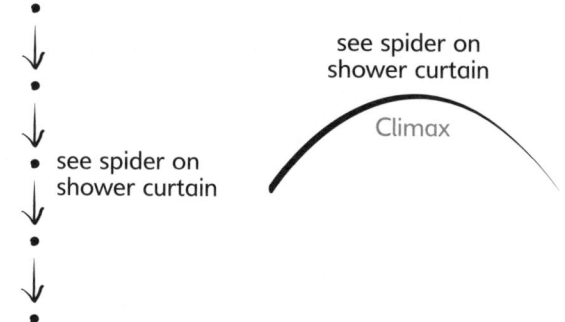

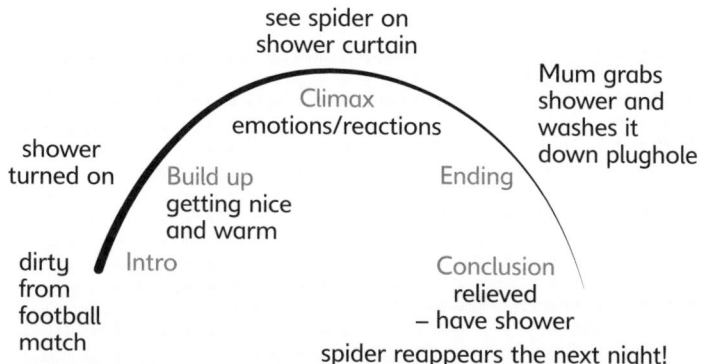

Although this plan uses five bullet points, your plan can include more if you need them. Each bullet point can relate to a corresponding paragraph or could just be a brief outline for a section that is made up of multiple paragraphs, depending on the type of text you're writing and how you like to plan.

 Create plans for stories with the following titles.

1. Panic at the Station
2. The Broken Statue
3. The Locked Door
4. The Accident
5. Voices in the Cupboard
6. The Secret Message

Schofield & Sims

Planning descriptive writing

As mentioned on page 106, a good description is like a telescope: you start with the big picture then zoom in on smaller details before zooming out again. Although small incidents may happen as part of the scene, no major events should happen in a description. You are not telling a story – you are just describing a scene as if you were painting a picture with words.

When you are planning the description, it helps if you take the same approach by starting with the general picture and then focusing in on specifics. You will then need to think about some general observations you can use for your conclusion.

Describe a busy train station.

First, brainstorm your ideas about things you may come across in a busy train station. Ensure that you engage all the senses – sight, hearing, touch, smell and taste – where possible.

Then, you can start to organise ideas into groups – the different people you might see, the different kinds of information you might encounter, the features of the trains, and so on.

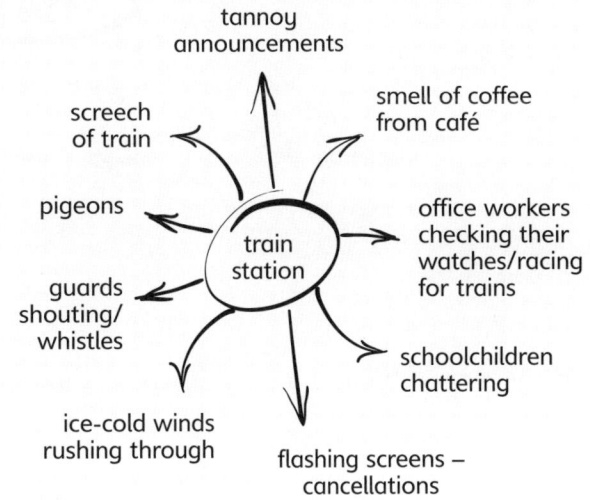

When planning the introduction, remember it is just setting a general scene and atmosphere, and answering questions such as who, what, why, where and when. The middle paragraphs are zoomed in on details and the conclusion is zooming out, giving a general atmosphere once again. However, the atmosphere can shift in the conclusion. It could be a different time of day, for instance.

- general hustle/bustle
  7 a.m. – rush hour
  wintery day/coffee smell/wind

   Introduction

- children/office workers/pigeons

   Detail 1

- announcements/groans/signs

   Detail 2

- finally – guard's whistle/shouting/
  train screeches in

   Detail 3

- zoom out – all is very quiet save
  for one pigeon & one guard rush
  hour is over

   Conclusion

 Create plans for descriptions with the following titles.

1. Picnic in the Summertime
2. At the Beach
3. Someone I Admire
4. In the Forest
5. The Museum
6. One Special Day

Planning non-fiction writing

Non-fiction takes a more essay-style approach, but you still need a brief plan. A plan will help you make sure you include plenty of informative or persuasive points and will help make sure your writing is well-balanced with a clear introduction, middle and conclusion. As before, always brainstorm ideas first.

Example one

Write a letter persuading your headteacher to add regular cookery lessons to the curriculum.

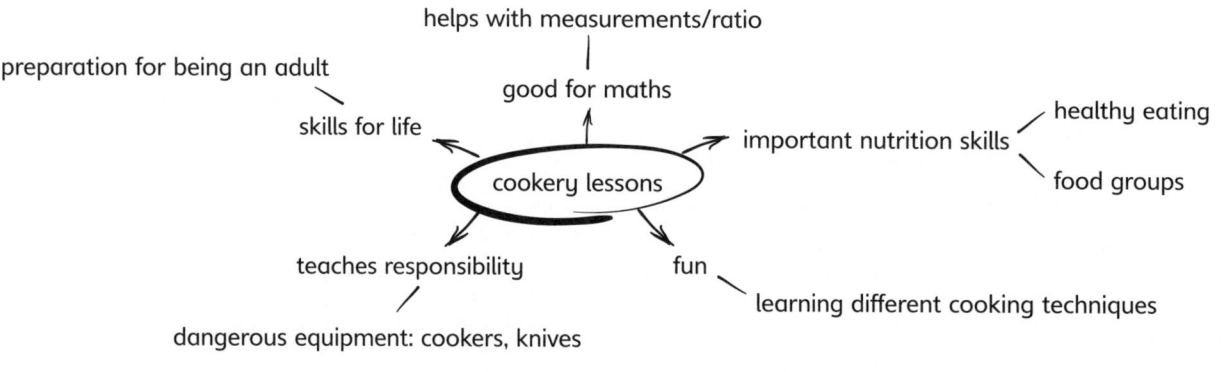

Example two

Write a speech encouraging others to support your favourite charity.

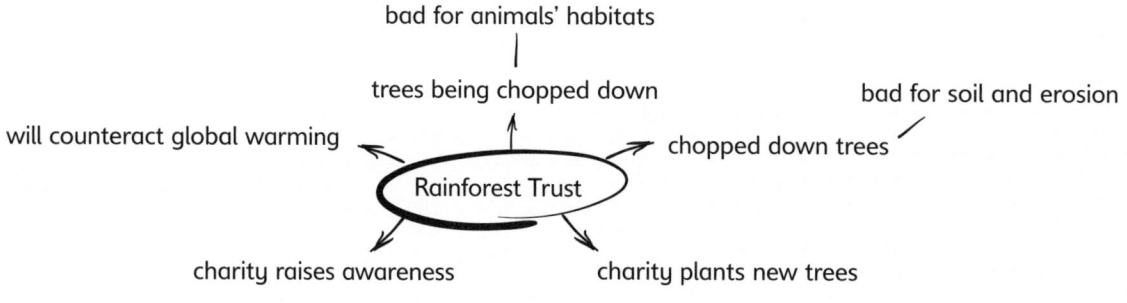

Example three

Write a diary entry as a treasure hunter discovering some treasure for the first time.

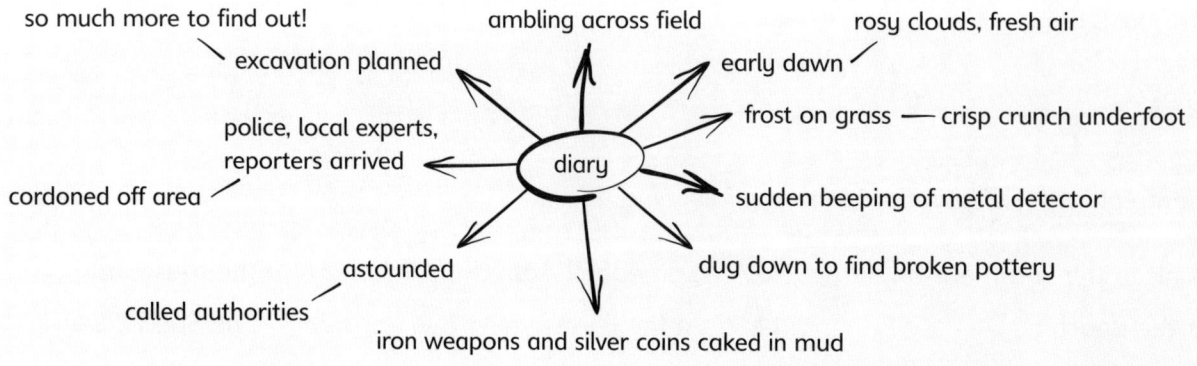

Schofield & Sims

Planning non-fiction writing

Most of the hard work is done – you just have to put your ideas into a logical order and include an introduction and conclusion. Remember – you set the scene in the introduction and conclude with thoughts on what will happen next, what you hope will happen next, or the next steps to be taken.

Example one

- Introduction: why I'm writing: discussions about healthy eating have led to pupils wanting more cookery lessons.
- Reason 1: good for maths: ratio, measures, etc. Statistics about children learning to cook.
- Reason 2: good for life skills: nutrition, meal planning, healthy eating. Rhetorical question.
- Reason 3: skills for the future: responsibility with dangerous equipment – emotive language.
- Conclusion: fun! I hope you will consider my reasons and conclude they are worthy of further discussion. Hope to hear from you soon.

Example two

- Introduction: everyone knows about the plight of the rainforest – trees being cut down, destruction of habitats, soil erosion. Rainforest Trust is the answer. Emotive language.
- Reason 1: plants new trees to help animals and the soil. Facts about animals' habitats.
- Reason 2: raises awareness and supports local communities with conservation work. Use emotive language.
- Reason 3: will rebalance global warming as trees breathe in CO_2. Statistics.
- Conclusion: my charity will make a real difference – by 2030, they could replant over one million trees with our support to reverse all damage done so far. Find out more. Donate. Rhetorical question.

Example three

- Introduction: what an eventful day! Finally found treasure after looking for it for months.
- Paragraph 1: went looking this morning – out at dawn. Early morning light, cold, frost under foot. Happy, but expecting it to be a normal day.
- Paragraph 2: metal detector started going off – excitement/anticipation – use similes. Describe digging for treasure and finding it.
- Paragraph 3: call authorities to report find. Sudden rush of activity, everyone excited. Becomes clear how important the find is.
- Conclusion: all very exciting! Everything went well – authorities grateful. Looking forward to finding out more about the site.

 TIP Your plan is like a set of instructions. Remember to indicate where you are going to describe important things and include emotions, reactions and literary techniques.

 Create plans for these non-fiction tasks.

1. Write a letter to your headteacher persuading them to let you introduce 'no-uniform' Fridays.

2. Write a speech encouraging your fellow pupils to do more to reduce climate change.

3. Write a newspaper report about the opening of a new leisure centre near your school.

4. Write a diary entry about an unexpected occurrence at your local park.

5. Write a letter of complaint to your local restaurant asking for your money back after an unsatisfactory meal there.

6. Write a diary entry as a famous person in history. Think about something special they may have done or experienced that day and write about their thoughts and feelings.

Improving your writing

Developing the detail

It is tempting to quickly jump from one idea or event to another when writing. However, it is often necessary to stick to one point for a few sentences so that your reader has time to process your idea.

For example, rather than describe a tree in one sentence, try to develop three or four sentences about it. This helps the reader develop a clearer picture of it and creates atmosphere:

> Towering trees stood proudly, as families on day trips wondered beneath them. Green leaves hung from their twisting branches like velvet cloaks from kings' shoulders. Their roots burrowed deep into the rich, damp earth. Crumbling pieces of cobwebbed bark tumbled to the forest floor in clumps, creating tiny mounds for woodlice to use as shelter.

When writing about someone's emotions, don't just state how they are feeling. Instead, give evidence to show they are feeling that emotion. Similarly, when writing about an action or event, add consequences of that action and other people's reactions:

> He skidded to a halt, his heart beating loudly in his chest. Everyone in the back seat sat motionless, too shocked to speak, their eyes wide with fear. All the other drivers had to brake quickly to avoid him and were now angrily beeping their horns. Slowly, the hedgehog shuffled across the road, oblivious to the chaos it had caused.

In non-fiction, it is very important to develop an idea fully before moving on:

> School uniform is an important part of a school's identity. When I walk down the street, I am proud to be wearing the coveted blue and red stripes of my school which reminds me of its rich and varied history. It helps me to bond with my fellow students and to feel part of something bigger, whose values and ethics I identify with.

 Write three to four sentences about each of the following, developing each detail thoroughly.

1. someone feeling angry

2. the weather changing from sunny to cloudy and gloomy

3. a rough sea

4. one point about why introducing sewing and knitting into the art curriculum is a good idea

5. a cat trying to pounce on a bird

Sometimes, developing detail can be tricky and you cannot think what to say next. If this happens, particularly in narrative writing, use the acronym **DEED?** to help you:

D – description – Dense grey clouds formed across the sky like a large cloak.

E – events – Amina shivered and looked around for her brother. He was nowhere to be seen.

E – emotions and reactions – Now she was scared. Her heart fluttered like a leaf in the wind and her hands shook. She rushed over to the platform where she had last seen him but he was gone. She began to cry large drops of salty tears.

D – dialogue – "Has anyone seen Tayyab?" she cried out. There was no reply.

? – question – Where had he disappeared to and how was she going to find him?

 Now answer the following question.

6. Use the acronym DEED? to write a paragraph about climbers stuck halfway up a mountain.

Schofield & Sims

Improving your writing

Improving your language

Use powerful verbs

Instead of using general verbs such as 'came' or 'said', be more precise so that your choice of words gives shades of meaning.

> Tiny ants **walked** across the leaf. → Tiny ants **scuttled** across the leaf.
> "Help!" she **said**. → "Help!" she **wailed**.

 Rewrite these sentences using more powerful verbs.

7. Large snowflakes fell from the sky.

8. She came in and shut the door.

Use emotive language

This means appealing to the emotions of the reader, which is especially useful in persuasive writing.

These adjectives make the rides sound far more dangerous.

Fun, **exciting** rides → **Thrilling**, **heart-stopping** rides

'These' makes the problem sound more personal and immediate.

These extra adjectives make you feel sorry for the animals.

The animals are **kept** in separate **kennels**. → **These poor, distressed** animals are **confined** to separate **cages**.

The word 'cages' sounds much worse than 'kennels'.

The word 'confined' sounds much more restrictive than 'kept'.

 Rewrite these sentences, adding emotive language or improving the words used.

9. I am annoyed at how many people are left alone at Christmas.

10. I would be happy if you would donate money to this good charity.

Use figurative language

If you are struggling with using figurative language, take a simple description and think about how you could use figurative language to say the same thing. A simile or metaphor works well if you want to show emotions.

 TIP Similes, metaphors and personification can help build a more vivid picture in the reader's mind. Look back at pages 88 to 91 for a reminder about the different types of figurative language.

> My cheeks **were red**. → My cheeks **glowed like tomatoes**.
> He **was angry**. → He **became a raging bull, stampeding around the playground**.

Personification works well with the weather and nature.

> There **was** an island in the lagoon. → The island **lounged comfortably** in the lagoon.

 Write sentences including figurative language about the following.

11. flags   12. clouds   13. flowers   14. lightning

Improving your writing

Including different types of sentences

As you know, there are four types of simple sentence – statement, question, exclamation and command. Over 90% of writing contains statement sentences only. This can get very dull and disengage the reader, so it is important to introduce other types of sentences into your writing. Look back at page 7 for more about the different types of sentence.

In narrative writing, different sentence types can be introduced successfully either by the narrator or through dialogue.

Questions: Where did the road lead? How many trees were there? Who was he? Who was following her? Was it safe? How did he escape?

Exclamations: What a mysterious house it was! How fast she could run! What a surprise it was to her!

Commands: Look further into the forest. Listen carefully to the birds. Imagine the scene. Meet Phillip.

There are opportunities to vary your sentence type when you are writing descriptive writing too. Sometimes, this might involve including sounds from the setting you're describing. You don't need to include all the sentence types, but thinking about different sentence types might help you to come up with some sounds to include. For this example, imagine you're describing a park.

Questions: "Can I have an ice cream?" "What type of bird is that?" "How much are the rowing boats?"

Exclamations: "What beautiful weather we're having!" "How nice it is to see you!" "How fast the dog is running!"

Commands: "Let me have a go on the swing." "Don't feed the ducks." "Look at the flowers."

Non-fiction writing works perfectly with other sentence types.

Questions: How can we continue to live like this? Who wouldn't want more free time? Who knows what the future brings? What can we do about it? When you hear the word 'homelessness', what do you picture?

Exclamations: How outrageous it is that we let people starve on the streets in this day and age! What an extraordinary decision!

Commands: Don't delay – book your free trial today. Imagine you were one of those poor defenceless people. Make your choice immediately. Think carefully about your decisions.

 Write a statement, question, exclamation and command about each of the following.

15. a mysterious door

16. two children arguing in a school playground

17. a town centre

18. a big race

19. making a negative point about the pollution emitted from a local factory

20. making a positive point about the benefits of making swimming lessons free to the under-fives

Schofield & Sims

Improving your writing

Varying sentence lengths

Sometimes, you need to stretch sentences to make them more engaging. You can do this by:

1. Extending noun phrases with extra detail.

The cat yawned. → The **large**, **vicious ginger** cat yawned.

longer, more detailed noun phrase

2. Adding an adverbial phrase or clause that gives extra information about where, when or how something happens. Explaining how, where or when something happens adds more detail, which makes the sentence more interesting for the reader.

fronted adverbial   adverbial clause

She received her award. → **Glowing with pride**, she received her award **while everyone cheered**.

3. Adding a subordinate or embedded clause to provide extra explanations, detail or reactions.

subordinate clause

The dog barked. → The dog barked **as it was scared by the little mouse**.
→ The dog**, which was being chased by the little mouse,** barked.

embedded clause

 Add an expanded noun phrase, adverbial or subordinate clause to these sentences.

21. The fish swam away from the shark.

22. The bear chased the hunters.

23. The crocodile is now safely back in its enclosure.

However, if all your sentences are long and complicated, this can also become dull and repetitive. You must break them up and develop excitement and tension through short sentences and sentence fragments. A sentence fragment is a group of words designed to give information but not in a complete sentence. You can use this technique in fiction or non-fiction.

This is a sentence fragment. The sentences around it are short sentences.

He stopped. He listened. **Nothing but silence.** Then the gun blasted.
Global warming. I hear that phrase and shudder. Ice caps melting. Polar bears suffering. This is what I picture.

By keeping the sentences short you speed up the pace, creating tension. You also emphasise dramatic pauses because a pause must take place every time a full stop is added.

 Write three to four short sentences and sentence fragments to build tension or emphasise a point dramatically about the following topics.

24. hearing a noise downstairs at night

25. the introduction to a speech about supporting an animal rescue charity

26. being chased

Varying sentence openers

If you constantly start sentences with determiners or the subject, the reader's mind will become bored and switch off. By varying the way you start a sentence, the reader will stay interested.

Here are a few other ways you could open sentences:

I – **–ing word** – '**Raging** with anger, he stormed out.'

C – **conjunction** – '**As** she watched, he focused intently.'

E – **–ed word** – '**Confused** and exhausted, she collapsed.'

A – **adjective** – '**Rich**, mellow music drifted across the room.'

S – **simile** – '**Like the wind**, she dashed across the field.'

A – **adverb** – '**Anxiously**, he called out.'

P – **preposition** – '**Above** the clouds, the majestic seagulls soared.'

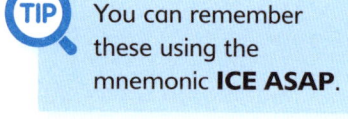 **TIP** You can remember these using the mnemonic **ICE ASAP**.

 Write sentences about the following topics using different ICE ASAP openers.

27. a description of a haunted castle

28. riding a roller coaster

29. screen time for young children

Varying your use of punctuation

Using a range of punctuation can have a powerful effect on your writing.

Dashes can be used for dramatic effect.

He stopped but felt nothing in the darkness – until a hand reached out to grab him!

They can also emphasise your point.

School uniforms are outdated and unfashionable – not to mention ridiculously expensive!

 Add a dash and extra information to these sentences.

30. She could feel something strange happening.

31. In the distance, smoke was rising.

32. The use of the library at lunchtime is invaluable to Year 6 pupils.

Semicolons and colons can be used to connect related information.

Rosa learnt to ski; Tom learnt to snorkel. ← The semicolon connects what was learnt by each person.

He was the last one to hear: he'd been asleep all morning. ← The colon connects the explanation to the effect.

 Add a semicolon or colon to the end of these sentences and add more information.

33. Everyone stood up and cheered

34. She felt much better

35. Hunting animals with dogs is cruel and violent

Writing mark scheme

You can use this mark scheme as a guide for what to look for and include in a piece of writing. You will notice that although content, sentences and language are only worth five marks each, collectively they are worth more than accuracy, as they are considered vital to the purpose and communication of the piece of writing. However, accuracy, although not worth as much as the other three together, is still necessary for understanding and expression. Therefore, it is weighted as $\frac{2}{5}$ of the whole mark.

Content and organisation	<ul><li>Does the task relate to the title?</li><li>Is it a sensible but interesting interpretation?</li><li>In stories, is there a clear climax with a balanced build up, resolution and conclusion?</li><li>Are ideas developed fully in each paragraph?</li><li>Have you paused to include description, where appropriate?</li></ul>	$\overline{5}$
Sentences	<ul><li>Have you used a range of sentences, including questions and exclamations?</li><li>Is your sentence length varied, including the use of short sentences and fragments?</li><li>Have you used embedded clauses and other devices to make your sentences varied?</li><li>Are your sentence openers varied? (ICE ASAP)</li><li>Have you included topic sentences at the beginning of each paragraph, where appropriate?</li></ul>	$\overline{5}$
Language	<ul><li>Have you used a range of language features to improve your writing, including: adjectives, verbs, similes, metaphors and personification?</li><li>Has formal language been used if appropriate?</li><li>Have you included emotive language and reactions where appropriate?</li><li>Have you used connectives as appropriate to move the action or ideas forward at the beginning of a paragraph?</li></ul>	$\overline{5}$
Accuracy	<ul><li>Is spelling of all common words accurate, with sensible attempts at more sophisticated vocabulary?</li><li>Is punctuation used accurately, including more sophisticated punctuation such as semicolons and dashes?</li><li>Are tenses consistent throughout?</li><li>Do you have correct subject-verb agreement?</li><li>Do your sentences make sense?</li></ul>	$\overline{10}$

Total marks are out of 25.

A good score for the grammar school 11+ would be 80% and over.

Now test your skills with these practice pages. If you get stuck, go back to pages 100 to 119 for some reminders.

 For each task, create a plan following one of the approaches described on pages 110 to 113. Then try to write at least one to one and a half pages.

1. Write a newspaper report with an appropriate headline about a gorilla escaping its enclosure at the local zoo.

2. Read this passage and then continue the story.

   It wasn't long before night fell. Danny and Clare knew they were lost. Danny thought something was wrong with the compass they had been given. They were supposed to be back at camp hours ago but that wasn't likely any time soon. Worse still, Clare was sure she could hear rustling behind them ...

3. Write a diary entry about the day you went on a boat trip with a surprising outcome.

4. Write a letter to a local councillor expressing your concern over increasing graffiti in the area and your ideas about how to address the issue.

5. Describe a surprising encounter – real or imagined – with an animal.

6. Write a letter as if you are an evacuee in World War II writing to your parents. Describe the first few days you've experienced so far.

7. You are presenting a speech to the school council on three changes that you think would make the school a better place. Write a speech outlining these three changes and try to persuade your fellow pupils that your ideas are the best.

8. Write a description using the picture below as a stimulus.

For each task, create a plan following one of the approaches described on pages 110 to 113. Then try to write at least one to one and a half pages.

1. You have been asked to write a letter of advice to a new pupil arriving at your school next term. Write a letter providing guidance on how to survive the first day and beyond.

2. Read the following abridged passage from *The Wind in the Willows* by Kenneth Grahame. Then continue the next part of the story, thinking about the mischief that Toad could get up to and the chaos he could cause.

Meanwhile, Toad, happy and irresponsible, was walking briskly along the high road, some miles from home.

Filled full of conceited thoughts he strode along, his head in the air, till he reached a little town, where the sign of 'The Red Lion', swinging across the road half-way down the main street,
5 reminded him that he had not breakfasted that day, and that he was exceedingly hungry after his long walk. He marched into the Inn, ordered the best luncheon that could be provided at so short a notice, and sat down to eat it in the coffee-room.

He was about half-way through his meal when an only too familiar sound, approaching down the street, made him start and fall a-trembling all over. The poop-poop! drew nearer and nearer,
10 the car could be heard to turn into the inn-yard and come to a stop, and Toad had to hold on to the leg of the table to conceal his over-mastering emotion. Presently the party entered the coffee-room, hungry, talkative, and gay, voluble on their experiences of the morning and the merits of the chariot that had brought them along so well. Toad listened eagerly, all ears, for a time; at last he could stand it no longer. He slipped out of the room quietly, paid his bill at the bar, and as soon as
15 he got outside sauntered round quietly to the inn-yard. "There cannot be any harm," he said to himself, "in my only just *looking* at it!"

The car stood in the middle of the yard, quite unattended, the stable-helps and other hangers-on being all at their dinner. Toad walked slowly round it, inspecting, criticising, musing deeply.

"I wonder," he said to himself presently, "I wonder if this sort of car *starts* easily?"

20 Next moment, hardly knowing how it came about, he found he had hold of the handle and was turning it. As the familiar sound broke forth, the old passion seized on Toad and completely mastered him, body and soul. As if in a dream he found himself, somehow, seated in the driver's seat; as if in a dream, he pulled the lever and swung the car round the yard and out through the archway.

Extract from **The Wind in the Willows by Kenneth Grahame.**

3. Write a diary entry about a day when you conquered a fear.

4. Write a story entitled 'The Lost Key'.

5. Write a newspaper report for your school magazine about the rise in popularity of a computer game and the problems it may cause.

Read the passage. Then choose **one** of the writing tasks to complete. Create a plan following one of the approaches described on pages 110 to 113. Then try to write at least one to one and a half pages.

1. Chris Hadfield is a retired Canadian astronaut who once commanded the International Space Station. He first went into space in 1995. In this extract from his autobiography, Chris describes the moment he heard he had been selected to be an astronaut.

When that Saturday finally arrived, I decided the best thing to do to make the time pass more quickly would be to go water-skiing with friends who had a boat, so that's what we did. Then Helene and I went back to the house to eat lunch and watch the clock. We figured they'd call the people they wanted to hire first, so if someone declined, they could move on to the next name on
5 the list. We were right: shortly after 1:00 the phone rang, and I picked it up in the kitchen. It was Mac Evans, asking if I wanted to be an astronaut.

I did, of course. I always had.

But my main emotion was not joy or surprise or even huge enthusiasm. It was an enormous rush of relief, as though a vast internal dam of self-imposed pressure had finally burst. I had not let
10 myself down. I had not let Helene down. I had not let my family down. This thing we'd worked toward all this time was actually going to happen. Mac told me I could tell my family, as long as they understood it needed to be kept entirely under wraps, so after Helene and I absorbed the news – insofar as we could – I called my mother and swore her to secrecy. She must have started phoning people as soon as she hung up. By the time I got my grandfather on the line, it was old
15 news.

Extract from **An Astronaut's Guide to Life on Earth by Chris Hadfield.** Text copyright © Chris Hadfield, 2013. Reproduced with permission of the Licensor through PLSclear.

i) Write a diary entry as if you are Chris Hadfield on the day of receiving the news.

ii) Write a letter as if you are Chris Hadfield sharing the news with a close friend.

iii) Write a newspaper article as if you are a reporter from Chris Hadfield's town sharing the news about his success.

iv) Write a letter as yourself to Chris Hadfield, asking him for details about his wonderful experiences in space and expressing your admiration for him.

v) Write a letter to NASA persuading them to give you a scholarship for their week-long space programme for young people to learn skills to be an astronaut.

Parents' notes

This book is divided into six sections, representing six key areas tested in 11+ English exams:

- grammar
- spelling
- comprehension
- punctuation
- vocabulary
- writing.

Each section contains explanations of English question types, as well as sets of practice questions. The book can therefore be worked through in its entirety, or you may select particular sections for your child to focus on.

If your child is sitting an 11+ exam set by CEM, the verbal reasoning sections of their exam may include some comprehension questions, which have been explained in this book. Explanations and examples of other verbal reasoning question types can be found in the **11+ Verbal Reasoning Study and Practice Book**, which is also available from Schofield & Sims.

Administering the Practice test

- When your child is confident answering each question type, they should sit the Practice test. This should be done in exam conditions, with an adult timing and marking the test.

- Before beginning the test, make sure your child has a pencil, an eraser and several sheets of rough paper. Also ensure that your child is able to see a clock or a watch.

- Advise your child to read each question carefully.

- Answers need to be written clearly. In some 11+ exams your child will be asked to rub out an incorrect answer, but in others they will be asked to cross it out. Explain to your child what to do if they make a mistake.

- Encourage your child to check their answers if they have time at the end of the test. This will also allow them to make sure that they haven't accidentally missed out any questions.

- The Practice test is divided by question type to allow you to identify any areas that your child has not yet understood.

- There is a time limit of 1 hour 30 minutes. When your child has finished the test, you should mark it using the answers section of this book and the Writing mark scheme on page 119. There are 150 marks available in total.

- The table below will help you to plan the next steps. However, these are suggestions only. Please use your own judgement as you decide how best to proceed.

Score	Time taken	Target met?	Action
1–119	Any	Not yet	Work through the explanation sections of this book again, ensuring that all question types are understood. If your child struggled with particular question types on the Practice test, focus on those sections.
120–150	Over the target – child took too long	Not yet	Use the appropriate age level **11+ English Rapid Tests** to improve speed.
120–150	On target – child took suggested time or less	Yes	Move on to **11+ English Rapid Tests** or **Progress Papers** to continue developing speed, accuracy and skill.

For further guidance on 11+ English exams, download the free **Parents' Guide to the 11+** from the **Schofield & Sims** website. This provides an overview of the exams and contains useful advice on organising your child's revision, as well as how to help them prepare for the day of the exam.

Practice test

Sentences, phrases and clauses

Identify whether these are phrases, main clauses or subordinate clauses.

1. A large, red ball _____

2. However lonely she felt _____

3. The dog barked menacingly _____

Identify whether this is a simple sentence, a compound sentence or a complex sentence.

4. Despite the driving rain and the fierce winds, the runners persevered to finish the marathon. _____

/4

Paragraphs

Use the paragraph symbol **/** before each word that should start a new paragraph in this passage.

5. Michelle Obama is a former First Lady of the United States and the wife of the 44th president, Barack Obama. She was also the first African American First Lady. Obama was born in Chicago on 17th January 1964. Having studied hard at school, she then attended Princeton University and Harvard Law School, after which she began a career in law. Michelle met Barack Obama at work. They got married in 1992 and have two daughters.

/2

Nouns

Complete the table using words from the sentence below.

6. Daniel looks after a swarm of bees, which takes great courage.

Common noun	
Proper noun	
Collective noun	
Abstract noun	

/4

Pronouns

 Rewrite the passage, replacing the repeated nouns with the appropriate pronouns.

7. The Wallace family enjoy playing games. The Wallace family particularly enjoy bridge, although Fabian, the oldest brother, always wins, whoever Fabian's partner is. Fabian is exceptionally competitive, and Fabian always makes sure the Wallace family follow the rules meticulously.

Underline the correct pronouns to complete the sentence.

8. Sophie was so pleased with *themselves / herself / ourselves* for passing her music exam

that she told all *her / his / hers* friends immediately.

/4

Practice test

Verbs

Underline the main verb or verbs in each sentence.

9.   As I drew the curtains, I noticed it was a beautiful sunny day.

10.   In the future, I hope that we will slow the rate of global warming.

Identify whether the verb in this sentence is in the past tense, the present tense or the future tense.

11.   Due to his very chatty friend, he was late for the bus.   _____

One verb has been used incorrectly in each sentence. Underline the incorrect verb and write the correct form of the verb on the line.

12.   Every Tuesday, I gone to classes at the youth centre.   _____

13.   Next week, my sister will took a very important driving test.   _____   /5

Active and passive sentences

Identify whether this sentence is active or passive.

14.   I was given the most beautiful watch by my auntie.   _____

Rewrite the active sentences in the passive voice and the passive sentences in the active voice.

15.   Frankie took the map that I needed out of my old, blue rucksack.

   _____

   _____   /2

Prepositions

Underline the preposition in the sentence. Then identify whether each one shows a location, direction or time relationship.

16.   In the night, a huge volume of snow fell.   _____

Choose the correct prepositions from the box below to complete each sentence. Use each preposition once.

17.

during	around	after	at	below

   i)   _____ a long drive, we arrived _____ the hotel.

   ii)   _____ winter, animals hibernate to escape the cold conditions.

   iii)   The diver swam far _____ her normal depth.

   iv)   I walked _____ the hole in the pavement.   /5

Adjectives

Identify whether these words are positive adjectives, comparative adjectives or superlative adjectives.

18. the loudest   _____

19. earnest   _____   /2

Adverbs

Underline the adverbs in each sentence.

20. The weather is extremely chilly today so I will need to wrap up warmly.

21. I am eating a very large piece of chocolate cake

which was cooked yesterday by my brother.

22. While Ty tried to sleep, loud thunder roared deafeningly

and blinding bolts of lightning flashed brilliantly.   /3

Connectives

Underline the connectives in the passage.

23. We would like to inform you that, although this evening's performance of *Cinderella* is

fully booked, we can offer you a seat in the mayor's box. This is a special honour as

nobody else has been offered this privilege. However, the mayor was particularly

impressed with all the charity work you do, so she suggested you be given this

opportunity. If you would like to book the seat, please contact the box office immediately.

Underline the connective that would complete each sentence in the best way.

24. *While / Through / Despite* the film was running, the projector stopped working.

25. That milk will go sour *if / for / unless* you put it in the fridge.

26. I will bring the washing in from the garden *in case / because / and* it starts to rain.   /5

Determiners

Underline the determiners in each sentence.

27. "Leave that box alone – it's her special present," said Annis.

28. Several bakers have exclaimed that this banana bread tastes wonderful.

29. Have you saved enough money to buy the jumper you like?   /3

Practice test

Sentence punctuation

Circle the punctuation mistakes in this passage.

30. what a strange day I've had As I was walking to school with Zainah, what do you think I saw. Out of nowhere, hailstones started falling. they weren't normal hailstones though – they were as big as Christmas puddings. We ran inside quickly. i wonder where they came from?

Circle the letter of the sentence that is punctuated correctly.

31. **A.** "Although it is snowing; I still want to go and weed the garden," Lupa said.

    B. Although it is snowing, I still want to go and weed the garden, Lupa said.

    C. "Although it is snowing, I still want to go and weed the garden," Lupa said.

    D. Although, it is snowing I still want to go and weed the garden." Lupa said.

/4

Commas

Circle any places in the passage where commas have been used incorrectly or are missing.

32. "If, you're going to the shop please get me some milk" Josie called out to Freya. Her list was already massive: bread, cheese eggs, pasta and sauce, cereal, bananas, and apples. She went back inside to get a bigger bag, but she nearly forgot her purse!

/3

Brackets and dashes

Use brackets to separate out the extra information in the sentence.

33. Lebkuchen a type of German biscuit are often eaten at Christmas.

Add the missing dash or dashes to each sentence.

34. The letter the one I sent last week has not been delivered yet.

35. It was the perfect result she won by a mile.

Cross out any brackets or dashes that are used incorrectly and add in any that are missing.

36. West Sussex a (county in England) is located on the south coast.

/4

Colons and semicolons

Add the missing colon to the sentence.

37. I missed Saran's 12th birthday party I was ill.

Add the missing semicolon to the sentence.

38. On Saturday, Femi went to football practice Jake stayed at home and watched a film.

/2

Hyphens

Add the missing hyphen or hyphens to the sentence.

39. Our much loved teacher retired at the age of sixty seven.

/1

Apostrophes

Add the missing apostrophes to the sentence.

40. Marcus dog couldnt find its favourite ball in the park, so Marcus asked the other owners if their dogs mightve taken it.

/2

Speech marks

 Rewrite the passage, adding the correct speech punctuation.

41. Have you seen that new movie set on Mars? asked Jensen. I thought it was really good. The other children smiled in agreement, except for Dylan. Perhaps he started it would have been better if there were fewer CGI effects. Some people nodded, yet others shook their heads. Yi commented that he liked how real the aliens looked. They scared me half to death! he added.

/3

Direct speech and reported speech

Turn this direct speech into reported speech.

42. Jessica asked, "Is this the page I need to complete my answers on?"

_____

Turn this reported speech into direct speech.

43. Max wanted to know when the match started as he hoped his team would win.

_____

_____

/2

Practice test

Singular and plural words

Underline the correct plural of the word that completes each sentence.

44. Elegantly, the *deers / deer / deeres* trotted across the path.

45. I always cut my *sandwiches / sandwich's / sandwitchis* into triangles.

Use the correct plural of the word in brackets to complete each sentence.

46. The _____ (wolf) howled at the top of their voices.

47. All the _____ (family) were waiting in line at the funfair.

/4

Root words, prefixes and suffixes

Underline the prefixes and suffixes which have been used incorrectly and then write out the correct version on the line.

48. It is inpolite to start eating while everyone else

is still waiting for their meal to be delivered. _____

49. Many people try to disprove the moon landing,

but I think they are disled. _____

Add the correct prefix or suffix to the word in brackets to complete the sentences.

50. It is a huge _____ (inconvenient) to have

to wait in all day for a delivery.

51. The runner _____ (easy) beat everyone and won the marathon.

Write the root word for each of these words.

52. unexpected _____

53. improperly _____

/6

Homophones

Write the correct word with the correct spelling for each meaning. The first letter of each word has been given to help you.

54. too proud of how you look   **v** _____

55. when something is given to you without charge   **c** _____

Underline the correct homophone of the word that completes each sentence.

56. He was given an eighteen *carrot / carat* gold ring but he *knew / new* it wouldn't fit.

57. The *stationery / stationary* cupboard was full of *grate / great* resources.

/4

Practice test

Spot spelling mistakes

Underline the spelling mistake in each sentence and then write out the misspelt word with the correct spelling.

58. It was necesary to redecorate the disgusting room. _____

59. Eva was desparate to win the important match. _____

Underline the correct spelling of the word that completes the sentence.

60. He was a very *mischievous / mischievious / mischiefous* dog. /3

Synonyms and antonyms

Underline the word on the right that means the same as the word in bold on the left.

61. moisture   mellow dampness most   **62. edge**   under tense margin

Underline the word on the right that is opposite in meaning to the word in bold on the left.

63. calm   happy tempestuous vigour   **64. emerge**   merge disappear open

Use the grid to answer the questions below.

65.

opulent	assemble	bewildered
perplexed	luxurious	lavish
convene	congregate	bemused

   i)   Find **three** synonyms for the word 'confused'.

     _____ _____ _____

   ii)   Find **three** antonyms for the word 'austere'.

     _____ _____ _____

Add the missing letters to the word on the right to make a synonym of the word on the left.

66. shrewd   __ s t __ t __   **67.** internal   __ n t __ r __ __ r

Add the missing letters to the word on the right to make an antonym of the word on the left.

68. copious   m __ __ g r __   **69.** diligent   __ n d __ l __ n __

70. Use the passage to answer the questions below.

For the end of year performance, we would like all pupils to participate. We encourage you all to audition and have the courage to try something new. We hope that this year's show will be the most extravagant ever.

   i)   Find a synonym in the passage for the word 'partake'. _____

   ii)   Find an antonym in the passage for the word 'modest'. _____ /16

Homonyms

Write **one** homonym to complete both sentences sensibly.

71. He needed a _____ to light the fire.

Her dribbling skills were no _____ for her rival.

72. They needed to keep up-to-date with the _____ situation.

The _____ was too strong to swim in.

Write the **one** word that has both meanings.

73. the directions on the front of an envelope

a type of formal speech _____

74. the noise made by a dog

the material covering a tree _____   /4

Cloze

Using each of the words in the box below once, complete the paragraphs by filling in the missing words.

75.

programming	later	human	woman	replacing
Committee	role	supervisor	early	successful

In the _____ years of the US space programme, the National

Advisory _____ for Aeronautics (NACA) did not have

machines to do their calculations. Instead, they relied on _____

mathematicians, who were called computers. Dorothy Vaughan joined the NACA as a

human computer and was promoted to be the _____ of the

West Area Computing unit in 1949. She was the first African American

_____ to take this _____.

When the NACA turned into NASA around a decade _____,

electronic computers were _____ human computers. Vaughan

joined NASA and learnt the _____ language FORTRAN. She

was a _____ computer programmer until she retired in 1971.   /10

Practice test

Abbreviations, acronyms and initialisms

Identify whether these are abbreviations, acronyms or initialisms.

76. VIP _____

77. radar _____

Give the full word or phrase for these abbreviations, acronyms and initialisms.

78. CD _____

79. dept. _____

/4

Compound words

Underline the **two** words, **one** from each group, that go together to form a new word.

80. (bat ball bored)   (room bath hit)

81. (see me no)   (ate went on)

Find **one** word that can be put in front of each of these words to make four new words.

82. grow   fit   law   wit   _____

83. room   sheet   stead   time   _____

/4

Comprehension

Read the following passage and answer the questions that follow.

84. One morning the Giant was lying awake in bed when he heard some lovely music. It sounded so sweet to his ears that he thought it must be the King's musicians passing by. It was really only a little linnet singing outside his window, but it was so long since he had heard a bird sing in his garden that it seemed to him to be the most beautiful music
5   in the world. Then the Hail stopped dancing over his head, and the North Wind ceased roaring, and a delicious perfume came to him through the open casement. "I believe the Spring has come at last," said the Giant; and he jumped out of bed and looked out.

What did he see?

He saw a most wonderful sight. Through a little hole in the wall the children had crept
10   in, and they were sitting in the branches of the trees. In every tree that he could see there was a little child. And the trees were so glad to have the children back again that they had covered themselves with blossoms, and were waving their arms gently above the children's heads. The birds were flying about and twittering with delight, and the flowers were looking up through the green grass and laughing. It was a lovely scene,
15   only in one corner it was still winter. It was the farthest corner of the garden, and in it was standing a little boy. He was so small that he could not reach up to the branches of the tree, and he was wandering all round it, crying bitterly. The poor tree was still quite covered with frost and snow, and the North Wind was blowing and roaring above it. "Climb up! little boy," said the Tree, and it bent its branches down as low as it could;
20   but the boy was too tiny.

Extract from **'The Selfish Giant'** by Oscar Wilde.

i) Why did the Giant think the music must be from the King's musicians?

_____ /1

ii) What does the word *casement* mean in line 6?

_____ /1

iii) Do you think that the Giant is glad that the Spring has come? Use evidence from the text to explain your answer.

_____

_____ /2

iv) ... *waving their arms gently above the children's heads.*

What does the word *arms* refer to in this sentence? Why do you think this word has been used?

_____

_____ /2

v) What do you think was creating the perfume that the Giant could smell?

_____ /1

vi) Do you think the little boy will get up into the tree? Use evidence from the text to explain your answer.

_____

_____

_____ /3

Writing

85. Choose **one** of these three tasks to complete.

i) Describe in **three** paragraphs, **three** different people at a busy train station.

ii) Think about the best holiday you have ever had. In **three** paragraphs, write about one particular day only.

iii) Write a letter to your teacher using **three** paragraphs. You want to persuade them to organise a trip to your favourite museum or place of historical interest.

/25

| **Total score:** | /150 | **Time taken:** | |

Grammar

Sentences, phrases and clauses (pages 6–7)

1. phrase
2. subordinate clause
3. main clause
4. phrase
5. main clause
6. subordinate clause
7. simple sentence
8. complex sentence
9. compound sentence
10. complex sentence
11. simple sentence
12. compound sentence

Paragraphs (page 8)

1. Poppy was excited about starting at her new school. She had just moved to a big city with her family and was hoping to make lots of new friends as soon as possible. **/** On her first day, she sprang out of bed before her alarm clock went off and headed downstairs for breakfast. She poured the cereal so fast that half of it jumped back out of the bowl and clattered on to the floor. **/** "Slow down!" said Mum. "School will wait." **/** "I just don't want to be late," replied Poppy as she ran upstairs to get dressed.

Nouns (page 10)

1.

Common noun	puppies
Proper noun	Fluffy
Collective noun	litter
Abstract noun	affection

2.

Common noun	leaves
Proper noun	Finley
Collective noun	pile
Abstract noun	enthusiasm

Pronouns (page 12)

1. During the summer, the Roberts family love to go on holiday to Dorset. **They** always stay in the same hotel, which is called the Sunflower Hotel. **It** is always busy, and Owen, the receptionist, is very friendly. **He** always greets all the guests with a smile and asks **them** how **they** are enjoying **their** stay.
2. Anything / **Everything** / Everyone has gone wrong today, so I can't leave work just yet.
3. This is the friend **who** / whom / which lives two doors down from me.
4. You will know that it is mine / theirs / **our** house as it has a bright red door.
5. The dog had a beautiful diamond collar around **its** / it's / him neck.
6. Anything / **Anyone** / Someone who wants to join the club should sign up today.
7. Please give **your** / hers / theirs completed forms to my / **me** / mine as soon as possible.
8. My friends and me / them / **I** would love to go swimming tonight.

Verbs (pages 13–16)

1. I **adore** my mother's deliciously sweet chocolate cake.
2. In the mornings, the birds up in the trees **sing** so loudly.
3. Sometimes I **catch** the bus to school with my friends despite the very long queue at the bus stop.
4. She **was** very tired yesterday due to an extremely long and busy day at the office.
5. In winter, heavy snowfall often **causes** severe delays to train services.
6. Today, I **went** to the park with my whole family and we **had** a picnic.
7. future
8. past
9. present
10. present
11. future
12. present
13. Last Christmas, I **giving** my friend a special present that I had made myself. **gave**
14. "Quick! Someone is **came**!" she shouted. **coming**
15. I will **got** lost if I do not take a map. **get**
16. The postal worker **delivers** a very strange parcel yesterday. **delivered**
17. "Where were you? I **sit** on my own for ages," he complained. **sat**
18. "**Made** sure you tidy up after you have finished cooking," demanded Shirley. **Make**

Active and passive sentences (pages 17–18)

1. active
2. active
3. passive
4. passive
5. active
6. passive
7. A deserted station was crashed into by a speeding train when its brakes failed.
8. My auntie gave me a very generous present last week.
9. My brother hurled a massive snowball at my little sister.
10. After dinner, a whole plate of biscuits was eaten by him.

Prepositions (pages 19–20)

1. The papers were scattered **around** the room. **location**
2. Everyone ran **towards** the bus stop. **direction**
3. The restaurant didn't open **until** noon. **time**

Answers

4. She hasn't completed any homework **since** Wednesday. **time**

5. He knew there was a special gift **inside** the box. **location**

6. **At** school, we had a wonderful surprise assembly. **location**

7.
  i) The horse jumped **over** the fence.
  ii) You must finish writing your letter **before** you eat your snack.
  iii) **During** playtime, she had to practise playing the piano.
  iv) It took all day for me to climb **up** the mountain.
  v) Hang the dress **inside** the wardrobe **next to** the orange skirt.
  vi) I will help you **in** a moment.
  vii) I am going to the park **with** my sister.
  viii) I must visit my uncle **at** exactly 10.00 a.m. **on** Thursday.

Adjectives (page 21)

1. superlative
2. positive adjective
3. superlative
4. comparative
5. comparative
6. positive adjective
7. superlative
8. comparative

Adverbs (page 22)

1. The bell rang **sonorously** – it would **soon** be time to go home from school. I was **really** **terribly** excited as it was my birthday and I was anticipating a warm welcome from my family when I got home. **Eventually**, after a long wait for my friend to catch up with me, we raced **merrily** down the street. I was thinking about the delicious chocolate birthday cake that I had baked with Dad **yesterday**. I couldn't wait to gobble it up **greedily** when I got home.

Connectives (page 24)

1. My grandfather died **before** I was born. **Since** he was a gentle man, he had enjoyed working as a nurse in a children's ward. I was told that he was also a proficient musician **and** could play several musical instruments.

2. *While* / *During* / *Since* I was doing my homework, a huge spider crawled across my desk.

3. Sienna was picked for the netball team *if* / **despite** / *because* only just returning from injury.

4. Deepak wanted cheese sandwiches for lunch *because* / *so* / **whereas** Darren wanted chicken salad.

5. She practised for many hours for her piano exam. *Nevertheless* / **As a result** / *On the other hand*, she passed with a mark of distinction.

Determiners (page 25)

1. **His** room was large and spacious with **many** bookcases and **enough** books squeezed on to them to fill **a** library!

2. I gave **every** orange-flavoured sweet I found to **my** sister.

3. Do you know if we have **any** pencils left in **the** stationery cupboard?

4. **Those** flowers are so beautiful and look perfect in **that** vase.

5. **Which** dessert would you like to choose from **this** delicious selection?

6. **An** angry customer charged through **the** shop like **a** raging rhinoceros.

Grammar practice page 1 (page 26)

1. phrase
2. subordinate clause
3. phrase
4. main clause
5. subordinate clause
6. main clause
7. simple sentence
8. complex sentence
9. simple sentence
10. complex sentence
11. complex sentence
12. compound sentence

13. It was the first day of term at Aleena's new school. She was thrilled to be starting Year 7 at Suchford Grammar. **/** At the bus stop, Aleena's friend Alex was already waiting for her. The bus arrived promptly, and they rushed to the back to chat with their other friends, who were already on the bus. **/** "I can't wait to see who my new teacher is," declared Aleena, and they all agreed that they were just so nervous and excited all at the same time. **/** As the bus approached the school, they could see a huge sign saying, 'Welcome Year 7'. Today was going to be a fantastic day!

14.

Common noun	flowers
Proper noun	Amaal
Collective noun	bouquet
Abstract noun	birthday

Grammar practice page 2 (page 27)

1. Jamil needed to buy some new shoes. **He** had just passed **his** music exam, so his mother let **him** pick the music in **her** car on the drive to the shop. **He** tried on a pair of trainers in **his** favourite colour. **He** exclaimed, "These feel great! They fit **me** perfectly!"

2. It was nice of **him** / *anybody* / *them* to bring *its* / **his** / *she* dog along to the park.

3. People **who** / *that* / *which* exercise regularly are normally quite fit.

Answers

Grammar practice page 2

(page 27) continued

4. No matter how hard I **try**, I **can't hit** the highest note of the song.

5. After a long day at school, I **jump** straight into a hot, bubbly bath.

6. Ever since I **was** young, I **have loved** watching game shows.

7. **present**

8. **future**

9. **past**

10. Yesterday, I went fishing and **catch** a huge fish that I took home and will cook for dinner tonight. **caught**

11. Normally, I like to watch my favourite TV programme in my bedroom, but today my family **sitting** in the lounge and enjoyed it together. **sat**

12. Next year, my sister wants to **went** to the sixth-form college near our house. **go**

13. Every Wednesday, I **played** hockey with my team and afterwards we all eat pizza together. **play**

Grammar practice page 3 (page 28)

1. **passive**

2. **active**

3. **active**

4. **The young amateur magician won the talent competition.**

5. **A delicious apple pie was baked by Sheila yesterday.**

6. **During** winter, it is important to wrap up warm. **time**

7. The world **beneath** the surface of the sea is truly fascinating. **location**

8. A solitary seagull soared **through** the clouds. **direction**

9. I will go to netball club **after** school. **time**

10. i) Megan and Logan shared the sweets **between** them.

 ii) He leant **against** the wall while he waited for his friend.

 iii) The hungry dog ran straight **past** his food, unaware of his mistake.

 iv) **After** dinner, we can watch your favourite programme if you like.

 v) All **through** the night he sat and listened to the sound of owls hooting.

 vi) Please wait **until** everyone has finished before you leave the table.

 vii) They climbed **up** the stairs and waited **on** the platform for the train.

Grammar practice page 4 (page 29)

1. **superlative**

2. **positive adjective**

3. **comparative**

4. **comparative**

5. **positive adjective**

6. **superlative**

7. Children **frequently** flock to the shop where Leona **regularly** sells misshapen sweets and broken chocolate bars for half price. The sweets are **very** popular. The **brightly** coloured wrappers enchant the children, and they can't wait to get their hands on the **eagerly** awaited prize.

8. I tried very hard to win the obstacle course, **but** I was unsuccessful. **After** I had managed to jump over the hurdles, I slipped **while** I was weaving through the cones. I ended up finishing behind everyone else. **However**, I didn't mind **because** I won the egg and spoon race!

9. _Despite_ / Since / As the cold weather, we decided to go for a long walk in the woods.

10. The cat meows enthusiastically wherever / **whenever** / as ever her owner returns.

11. I would love to be a vet when I grow up **as** / so / although I've always enjoyed helping animals.

12. The grass has grown very long, since / **so** / because I will have to mow the lawn later.

13. **These** snacks look delicious – I am going to take **two** biscuits.

14. **Whose** socks are lying all over **the** floor?

15. Do you know where **the** folder is that I left on **the** table?

16. Do you have **enough** money for **that** fairground ride?

17. **My** cousin gave me **an** elegant green dress for Christmas.

Punctuation

Sentence punctuation (page 32)

1. at the beach in brighton, hundreds of families were enjoying their summer holidays children were splashing in the sea, and robert and Jane were snorkelling. What more could anyone wish for Suddenly, there was a scream. "Help Help I've lost my watch" cried a child Luckily, someone dived down to the seabed to retrieve it.

 **A**t the beach in **B**righton, hundreds of families were enjoying their summer holidays. **C**hildren were splashing in the sea, and **R**obert and Jane were snorkelling. What more could anyone wish for? Suddenly, there was a scream. "Help! Help! I've lost my watch!" cried a child. Luckily, someone dived down to the seabed to retrieve it.

2. **B**

Commas (page 34)

1. "On your marks**,** get set**,** go!" called out Ms Grover. As the race started**,** Rose zoomed out in front while Jamie followed close behind. They were almost neck and neck. Suddenly**,** Erin**,** who had stumbled at the start**,** appeared**,** and she overtook them both.

2. Although he was an old dog⊘ Joe acted like⊘ a puppy. He loved playing fetch for hours⊘ he gobbled⊘ down his food in seconds and he tried to sit⊘ in Zack's lap. "Come on, Joe**,**" said Zack⊘ "get down! You're far too big for that."

Brackets and dashes (pages 35–36)

1. Jaguars **(**a type of big cat**)** are highly effective predators.

2. My favourite author **(**Roald Dahl**)** wrote more than 30 books.

3. Put your date of birth **(**D.O.B.**)** in the correct format on your passport form.

4. She was too short **(**99cm**)** to go on the ride.

5. The weather was going to be perfect all day **–** or so we thought.

6. The book that I'm reading **–** *Treasure Island* by Robert Louis Stevenson **–** is about pirates.

7. The school trip **–** a visit to the *Mary Rose* **–** was a huge success.

8. Everything was lovely and peaceful in the house **–** then my little cousin turned up!

9. Mr Webb **–** he teaches me maths **–** is an excellent golfer and has won several trophies.

10. We will be arriving into London⊘ (Heathrow)⊘ (LHR) at 3.00 p.m.

11. Vipers (a type of⊘ snake) are very poisonous.

12. Andy Murray – a British⊘ tennis player – has won Wimbledon twice.

13. The play was about to⊘ start – then a member of the audience fainted!

Colons and semicolons (pages 37–38)

1. At 4.00 p.m., the judges' verdict was announced**:** Emilia had won the competition.

2. When he looked in the cage, it dawned upon him**:** the hamster had escaped!

3. Lin purchased the decorations for her party**:** balloons, streamers and banners.

4. On Monday, the drama teacher's choice for the school production was announced**:** the students would perform *Alice in Wonderland*.

5. I had lots of different fruits for breakfast this morning**:** banana, apple, kiwi, pear and mango.

6. It was a lovely sunny day**;** it seemed as if the whole town had decided to go for a walk.

7. Nisha received so many presents: a red, yellow and orange pencil case**;** a jumper with a snowman on it**;** a new bell for her bike**;** and a poster of her favourite singer.

8. Rhys starts school on Tuesday**;** Lacey starts school on Thursday.

9. At the award ceremony, the actor thanked his agent for getting him fantastic roles to play**;** his mother, who drove him to all his classes as a child**;** his acting coach for all the good advice he gave**;** and his loyal fans.

10. It is important to eat a balanced diet**;** it is also beneficial to exercise regularly.

Hyphens (page 39)

1. The dessert contained mouth-watering mango and chocolate-covered strawberries.

2. Five hundred and twenty-eight people were saved from the deadly avalanche.

3. The election was flawed, so the ex-Prime Minister asked for a recount.

4. The car has a state-of-the-art design and is available from mid-May.

5. After the freezing-cold night, the windscreen had to be de-iced.

Apostrophes (pages 40–41)

1. **a**
2. **a**
3. **o**
4. **wi**
5. **u**
6. **ha**
7. **the boy's jumper**
8. **Lois's bike**
9. **the ants' nest**
10. **the geese's pond**

11. It's fortunate that warm weather is forecast for the day of the spring picnic.

12. Charles' favourite game was chess. (*Charles's is also correct but requires the addition of an extra 's'.*)

13. I wasn't sure whether six hours would be sufficient to see all the animals in the wildlife park.

14. Isn't it amazing that snakes shed their skin every few months?

15. Sally suddenly realised that she'd left her coat at her children's school.

Speech marks (page 43)

1. It was time for the weekly multiplication test.

   "Who**,**" asked Mrs Taylor**,** "can tell me what the product of 7 and 8 is**?**" Everyone looked bewildered.

   "I don't know what a product is**,**" said Angel bravely**.** "I've never heard that word before**.**"

   Kwame piped up cheerfully**,** "I know what it is**!** It is when you multiply one number with another number**,**" he announced confidently.

Answers

Direct speech and reported speech
(page 44)

1. **Flavia said that it was late and that she needed to catch her bus.**

2. **Shivesh said that no matter how hard he tried, he couldn't play tennis very well.**

3. **Mr Spencer claimed that if you work hard, you will succeed.**

4. **"Can I join the football club after Christmas?" asked Daisy.**

5. **"It's getting very dark outside and it might rain," noticed Aaron.**

6. **"When is your birthday, Tiana?" asked Veronica.**

Punctuation practice page 1 (page 45)

1. I am reading a very exciting book at the moment called(swallows and(amazons.

   *I am reading a very exciting book at the moment called **S**wallows and **A**mazons.*

2. Is the start of the holidays today or tomorrow!

   Is today the start of the holidays, or is it tomorrow?

3. That is an amazing test score – well done?

   That is an amazing test score – well done!

4. I am hoping that I can finish my homework quickly() It is my birthday tomorrow.

   I am hoping that I can finish my homework quickly. It is my birthday tomorrow.

5. **D**

6. **C**

7. Anxiously, the waiter carried the soup out, hoping not to spill it.

8. "Lily-Mae, I hope that you can come to my party next week."

9. Without any warning, the hurricane changed course and swept into Florida.

10. I need to buy, a fountain pen, colouring pencils, and a selection of paints.

11. Deep, in the dark, gloomy forest stood a tall, towering tree.

12. Reluctantly, she realised, that she would have to admit defeat.

13. "I wish, she moaned, "that I was just a little, bit taller!"

Punctuation practice page 2 (page 46)

1. Chameleons (famous for camouflaging themselves) can be found living in the rainforests of Madagascar.

2. The puppy (21 weeks old) was found hiding behind a neighbour's toolshed.

3. Please reply ASAP (as soon as possible) in order to get your tickets.

4. Diwali (the festival of light) is celebrated in either October or November.

5. Everyone thought the tiger had been captured – except the zookeeper!

6. All students – including sixth-formers – must attend school in uniform.

7. The sky was pitch-black – not a star could be seen for miles.

8. Tasmania – an island off the south coast of Australia – is known for its many exotic creatures, such as the Tasmanian devil.

9. My older sister (Louise) has just trained as a yoga teacher.

10. I cannot believe it – I have seen four lightning strikes in a row.

11. We made a birthday cake (chocolate fudge) for my party.

12. The juggler threw seven balls in the air – then dropped them all!

13. My pet dog – named Buster – is going to be twelve years old soon.

14. It is very worthwhile learning to play an instrument (especially the drums or piano) as it helps develop co-ordination.

15. The results were revealed in reverse order: Jian had received third prize.

16. It wasn't long before he realised his mistake: he had taken the wrong turn at the last junction.

17. On Monday morning, the classroom was sweltering: somebody had left the radiator on over the weekend.

18. The atmosphere was tense; nobody wanted to leave the auditorium in case they missed hearing who had won.

19. It is very hard to learn another language; some people try for years.

20. On holiday, I would like to try snorkelling with turtles; whale watching in a glass-bottomed boat; sailing; and perhaps surfing as well.

21. It was a beautiful day; everyone was enjoying the unusually warm weather.

Punctuation practice page 3 (page 47)

1. The record-breaking athlete trained extremely hard every day.

2. Sixty-seven people from our town joined the protest on Saturday.

3. The space shuttle vibrated violently on re-entry to Earth's atmosphere.

4. The first few years in post-apartheid South Africa were a time of great hope.

5. Heather's gift was a beautiful, satin-lined coat.

6. The president-elect will not take office until mid-January.

7. As the actor thought about the ninety-seven people in the audience, he was suddenly stricken with fright.

8. Lots of well-known rock bands became famous in the 1960s.

9. "That sofa is so filthy! It definitely needs re-covering."

10. My new flat has a well-equipped kitchen with lots of modern gadgets.

11. It doesn't feel like winter as the weather is so warm!

12. I am hoping that the parents' evening won't last too long as I am starving!

13. Willa's favourite animal is her pet rabbit because its fur is so soft.

14. The children's party at my house is going to be very chaotic – I will need everyone's help.

15. It's cute when the excited dog wags its tail expectantly, hoping for a large, juicy bone.

16. Most cakes contain cow's milk and other dairy produce.

17. The babies' toys were scattered all over the floor, but their parents weren't the least bit concerned.

18. He walks his own dog every day but doesn't ever notice any other dogs in the park.

19. I won't go to netball practice today as they're only practising passing and I prefer shooting.

20. The women's rugby team hasn't lost a game in two seasons!

Punctuation practice page 4 (page 48)

1. "Do you think," said Chloe, "that the interview is here?"

2. "Can I come in and look at your new piano?" asked Ivan.

3. "Don't go near the water as there are lots of jellyfish!" shouted Naomi.

4. Aunty Marion said, "Come here, I want to see how much you have grown."

5. "Can I check," asked Danielle, "whether that's my jumper?"

6. "Run!" shouted Mark. "The dog is after us!"

7. **Alys said to Jerome that she was ever so sorry to hear that he had been unwell.**

8. **Deborah said, with a smile, that it would be great if they won the lottery this weekend.**

9. **Mr Patel shouted to the children that they must not forget to bring a packed lunch for the trip.**

10. **"Do not leave the room without my permission," Ms Davis told the class.**

11. **"The queue was so long that I couldn't see the end!" an eyewitness remarked.**

12. **"It was a very enjoyable concert, although it was too loud," said a spectator.**

Spelling

Singular and plural words (page 50)

1. The football team for womans / <u>women</u> / woman are having a very successful season.

2. We learn to use knifs / knive's / <u>knives</u> safely in cookery class.

3. There are lots of damaged <u>trolleys</u> / trolles / trollys in the supermarket car park.

4. We need more <u>cellos</u> / celloies / cello's in the string section of our orchestra.

5. **foxes**

6. **fish**

7. **flies**

8. **tomatoes**

Root words, prefixes and suffixes
(pages 53–54)

1. I am so <u>gratement</u> for the help that I have received. **grateful**

2. It was <u>imfortunate</u> that I lost my keys on the train. **unfortunate**

3. I <u>disjudged</u> how long the cake needed to bake. **misjudged**

4. My new kittens are so cuddly and <u>lovible</u>. **lovable/ loveable**

5. One <u>superordinary</u> day, a surprise visitor came to school. **extraordinary**

6. The weather was very changeable – sun then <u>torrencial</u> rain. **torrential**

7. **studious**

8. **loneliness**

9. **defrost**

10. **curiously**

11. **foresee**

12. **normality**

13. **comfort**

14. **heat**

15. **appreciate**

16. **hurry**

17. **faith**

18. **cook**

19. **plant**

20. **satisfy**

Homophones (page 55)

1. **allowed**   2. **prophet**   3. **whole**

4. A ravenous eagle circled *hire* / **higher** above its **prey** / *pray* before swooping down to catch it.

5. The berry tasted **sweet** / *suite* and was full of sticky **red** / *read* juice.

6. The *fair* / **fare** for the bus has increased *to* / **too** much in recent years.

Spot spelling mistakes (page 59)

1. The painting was an **origanal** by Monet and was considered priceless. **original**

2. Roaring **fearcely**, the lion ran away from the poachers. **fiercely**

3. The **dessert** was surprisingly cool at night. **desert**

4. They decided to **seperate** the players into an A team and a B team. **separate**

5. A **freind** of mine was just saying how much fun playing tennis is. **friend**

6. Jacob's online **busness** was becoming very successful. **business**

7. A *squirell* / *squirel* / **squirrel** scampered across the roof and into the oak tree.

8. Did you hear that *wierd* / **weird** / *weerd* noise a moment ago?

9. The more I *practice* / **practise** / *praktice*, the better I will be.

10. When I returned the clothes, the cashier asked for my **receipt** / *reciebt* / *receit*.

Spelling practice page 1 (page 60)

1. How many *loafs* / *loavs* / **loaves** of bread are there in the oven?

2. This soup contains *potatos* / **potatoes** / *potatows*, carrots, peas and leeks.

3. The **witches** / *witchis* / *whiches* cackled menacingly as they gathered around the cauldron.

4. The chefs had lots of spices on their *shelfes* / **shelves** / *shelvs*.

5. I can hear *mouses* / *mices* / **mice** scuttling around in the attic.

6. The farmer brought his **sheep** / *sheeps* / *sheepes* into the barn for the winter.

7. Our resort is the ideal holiday destination for **families** / *familys* / *family's*.

8. The chimney sweep paused for a moment to look out over the *roofes* / *roovs* / **roofs**.

9. **tragedies**   11. **stimuli**   13. **scarves**

10. **teeth**   12. **donkeys**   14. **dominoes**

Spelling practice page 2 (page 61)

1. It was very **antiresponsible** of you to walk across that busy road. **irresponsible**

2. I had to **overheat** the oven before I put the cake inside. **preheat**

3. The fairy lights added a **magiciful** touch to the room. **magical**

4. Sorry, but I **disunderstood** the question. **misunderstood**

5. Everyone else was very excited about the trip, but Sammy was **imdifferent**. **indifferent**

6. She was the **youngous** girl in the class by two months. **youngest**

7. We had to call the **electritian** as all the lights went out. **electrician**

8. Henna was **grateness** for the help she got with tidying the classroom. **grateful**

9. He was perfectly **capible** of completing his homework, but he refused. **capable**

10. **dishonest**   17. **computerise**

11. **submarine**   18. **music**

12. **comfortable**   19. **decide**

13. **different**   20. **terror**

14. **combustible**   21. **connect**

15. **direction**   22. **thank**

16. **international**   23. **encourage/courage**

Spelling practice page 3 (page 62)

1. **hare**   3. **hymn**   5. **cereal**   7. **coarse**

2. **sole**   4. **heir**   6. **scent**   8. **tow**

9. "Dad's ice cream van *past* / **passed** the MOT!" shrieked Paula.

10. The fight **scene** / *seen* in the new action film was extremely exciting!

11. Please do not *waist* / **waste** food from the canteen – take less if you are not hungry.

12. I am a *guessed* / **guest** at an extremely important event tonight.

13. Please may I have an extremely small *peace* / **piece** of chocolate cake?

14. The train was **stationary** / *stationery* on the platform for quite some time.

15. The **sealing** / *ceiling* on the envelope came loose and everything fell out.

16. Drinking coffee late at **night** / *knight* can have strange side *affects* / **effects**.

Answers

17. My aunt _made_ / maid me some shorts but they were _too_ / two long so I had to _alter_ / altar them.

18. The _site_ / sight of the wreckage was not far from the coast, just beyond the key / _quay_.

Spelling practice page 4 (page 63)

1. Mackenzie loved to play tennis, **acording** to her friend, Jasper. **according**

2. My auntie cooked a delicious **vegatable** curry when I visited her. **vegetable**

3. I **sensably** decided to make a plan before beginning my project. **sensibly**

4. Who is **definately** coming to my party later this month? **definitely**

5. As well as fireworks, my cats are extremely frightened of **lightening**. **lightning**

6. I will be **completly** ready for the competition next week after this last rehearsal. **completely**

7. Algebra is **basicly** learning to problem-solve with numbers and letters. **basically**

8. I need to mark on my **calender** when all my friends' birthdays are so that I don't forget them. **calendar**

9. The library's _reference_ / refference / referance section was useful for my project on local history.

10. The house was hansome / _handsome_ / handsom and had been well looked after.

11. As she was a very _careful_ / carful / carefull chess player, she beat many opponents.

12. Our new puppy (a cute yellow Labrador) is very exciteable / exiteable / _excitable_.

13. The _miserable_ / misrable / miserible builder cheered up when the rain stopped.

14. My neihbour / nieghbour / _neighbour_ is an extremely good musician.

15. I waved enthusiasticly / enthusiasticaly / _enthusiastically_ so my friend would see me in the crowd.

16. Would you like to go to the cinema tomorow / _tomorrow_ / tommorrow?

Vocabulary

Synonyms and antonyms (pages 64–68)

1. leave

2. conflict

3. achieve

4. decrease

5. competent

6. hard-working

7. bewilder

8. carry

9. partial

10. bold

11. agitated

12. rude

13. starve

14. stern

15. important

16. hostile

17. i) persuade, assure, sway
ii) fortunate, blessed, lucky

18. plentiful

19. combine

20. kingdom

21. peaceful

22. heroic

23. snooze

24. dismantle

25. tranquil

26. punish

27. serious

28. flexible

29. fail

30. i) desolate
ii) come across
iii) heavy
iv) tiny

31. i) enough
ii) lucky
iii) abundant
iv) delicate

Homonyms (pages 69–70)

1. bear

2. patient

3. pupils

4. handle

5. jam

6. loom

7. can

8. down

9. wave

10. tender

11. spring

12. bat

13. remote

14. trip

Cloze (page 71)

1. Peregrine falcons are large birds of **prey** found on all continents except Antarctica, where the **habitat** is too hostile. You can easily **distinguish** them from other birds as they have a distinctive greyish-blue back, white underbelly and a black head. They are **superior** hunters whose highly developed agility and **eyesight** mean they can prey on other birds and bats in mid-flight. When a peregrine falcon spots its prey, it will **swoop** down in a dive that can reach up to 200mph. This makes it the fastest in the animal **kingdom**.

Abbreviations, acronyms and initialisms (page 72)

1. acronym

2. abbreviation

3. initialism

4. acronym

5. advertisement

6. United Kingdom

7. as soon as possible

8. application

Compound words (page 73)

1. (**know** think like) (help **ledge** slip) (knowledge)

2. (shield dagger **spear**) (moss grass **mint**) (spearmint)

3. (**by** me lay) (wall path **pass**) (bypass)

4. tea (teasing, teacup, tearing, teapot)

5. wind (windmill, windsurf, windswept, windscreen)

6. sea (season, seafront, seahorse, seashell)

Answers

Vocabulary practice page 1 (page 74)

1. genuine
2. merry
3. ample
4. dwindle
5. i) obstruct, hinder, thwart
   ii) fearless, extroverted, unabashed
6. tiresome
7. postpone
8. vivid
9. colossal
10. i) working
    ii) pail
    iii) penetrating
11. i) discontent
    ii) weary
    iii) bolted

Vocabulary practice page 2 (page 75)

1. mould
2. fiddle
3. break
4. hide
5. rich
6. record
7. well
8. pen
9. rose
10. trunk
11. digest
12. fine

Vocabulary practice page 3 (page 76)

1. Chameleons are a beautiful type of **lizard** that are mostly found on the **continent** of Africa. There are over 150 different **species**. Many of these have the **ability** to change colour, which helps them to increase or decrease their temperature, to communicate with other chameleons or to blend in with their **surroundings**.

   Chameleons have some distinctive physical features. In particular, their toes – two of which face forward and two of which face backward – assist their **grip** and agility. They also have long, thin, **extending** tongues and eyes that are independently **mobile** to give them a wide view of their surroundings.

2. No one would have **believed** in the last years of the nineteenth **century** that this world was being watched keenly and closely by **intelligences** greater than man's and yet as mortal as his own; that as men busied themselves about their various concerns they were **scrutinised** and studied, perhaps almost as narrowly as a man with a microscope might scrutinise the transient creatures that swarm and **multiply** in a drop of water. With infinite **complacency** men went to and fro over this **globe** about their little **affairs**, serene in their assurance of their empire over matter.

Vocabulary practice page 4 (page 77)

1. initialism
2. initialism
3. acronym
4. abbreviation
5. acronym
6. abbreviation
7. do it yourself
8. telephone
9. personal identification number
10. estimated time of arrival

11. absent without leave
12. luncheon
13. (**sun** sky wind) (flight **shine** dark) (sunshine)
14. (before during **after**) (night **noon** morning) (afternoon)
15. (help **leader** male) (**ship** full lace) (leadership)
16. (**life** live love) (hood **boat** mate) (lifeboat)
17. (mouth arm **tooth**) (save board **pick**) (toothpick)
18. (**eye** ear toe) (net bat **ball**) (eyeball)
19. (**man** sit will) (**age** now tone) (manage)
20. (**near** all hang) (on **by** met) (nearby)
21. **be** (become, beat, behave, beam)
22. **to** (totally, tonight, towed, today)
23. **can** (cannot, canteen, candid, candies)
24. **with** (withdraw, withhold, withstand, within)
25. **her** (herself, heron, herring, herding)
26. **key** (keypad, keyhole, keyword, keyboard)

Comprehension

Identifying text types (pages 79–81)

1. adventure fiction
2. historical fiction
3. fantasy fiction
4. fairy tale
5. newspaper report
6. diary
7. instructions
8. information/reference text
9. biography
10. brochure/leaflet

Retrieving information from texts (page 83)

1. (*Accept anything that identifies key aspects of who, what, where, when, how and why.*)

   Martin Luther King Jr was born in **Atlanta, USA** on **15th January 1929**. In the **1950s**, he became a **leading activist and spokesperson in the civil rights movement**, which protested against **racial discrimination in the southern American states**. As a Baptist minister, he promoted **non-violent protests**, including marches and acts of civil disobedience. This approach was partly inspired by the work of **Mahatma Gandhi** in India, but also reflected his **own religious beliefs**.

2. i) Their **screeches** are the thing that is particularly disturbing about a Tasmanian devil.
   ii) Their **ferocity** is evident when they are feeding.
   iii) Their **large head and mighty jaws** give Tasmanian devils their powerful bite.

Schofield & Sims

Answers

3. i) She is in **a forest**.

    ii) She had been **walking through the forest since dawn**.

    iii) There was a **fire** in the village that was going to **burn everything**.

    iv) She sees and hears **woodpeckers**, **squirrels** and **hedgehogs**.

    v) She needs to find shelter soon because **dark clouds** are **looming**, the **sun** is **lowering** and the **temperature has dropped**.

Using inference and deduction (page 85)

1. i) **The passage is set in winter.**

    ii) **They are going to go ice-skating on the lake, which has frozen over.**

    Answers could include the following points:

    iii) **Lottie, because Lottie owns two pairs of ice-skates, so she has probably gone ice-skating lots before, but Nadia needed to borrow a pair. Also, Nadia is more nervous than Lottie, so she seems less experienced.**

    iv) **Lottie is feeling happy and excited because she 'chattered' and is 'grinning'.**

    v) **Nadia seems nervous, but she also seems excited and determined to go ice-skating. She 'chattered' with Lottie at the start, so she is excited, but then her heart is 'fluttering like a hummingbird' and she hesitates before saying she is ready, which makes it seem like she is nervous. She doesn't hesitate for long though, so she also seems determined to start.**

2. *Answers could include the following points:*

    Fawn Sprocket is critical because she has 'judging eyes'. People want to avoid her, so it seems like she is usually unfriendly. She is also unsociable and rude because she just gives 'a sniff and a grunt' instead of saying 'Good morning' when people go past her.

Identifying word meanings (page 87)

1. **like a palace/spacious/luxurious**

2. **sorry/showing remorse**

3. **unimportant/unnecessary**

4. **boldness/cheek/rudeness**

5. **hard/physical/tiring**   6. **secretly/stealthily**

Literary techniques (page 91)

1. **idiom/cliché**   2. **metaphor**   3. **proverb**

4. **alliteration and personification**

5. **personification and onomatopoeia**

6. **euphemism**   7. **oxymoron**   8. **irony**

9. **rhetorical question**   10. **onomatopoeia**

Comprehension question types (page 93)

1. **C**

2. **The atmosphere on the street was hostile because of the cold. The narrator says that 'The cold became intense' and the water-plug 'turned to misanthropic ice', which shows that it felt horrible to be outside.**

    However, the atmosphere was at the same time jolly. It says that some workers gathered around a great fire, 'warming their hands and winking their eyes before the blaze in rapture'. The shops are bright, and the narrator describes them as 'a splendid joke' and 'a glorious pageant', which suggests Christmas cheeriness. People are going out to prepare for Christmas in the streets from the Lord Mayor's household to the tailor's household, so the atmosphere must also be quite busy. *(Award 1 mark for each point about the atmosphere up to a maximum of 2 marks. Award 1 mark for each piece of evidence from the text up to a maximum of 2 marks. Award 1 mark for each explanation demonstrating how the evidence supports the point up to a maximum of 2 marks. Maximum 6 marks.)*

Comprehension practice page 1 (page 95)

1. **Night came early as it was winter and daylight lasts a short time in winter.**

2. **The word 'toiled' means walked/travelled with effort/difficulty.**

3. **erect**

4. **One Ear, because Henry says the stick is the 'only contraption that'll ever hold One Ear', which suggests that the men are most worried about One Ear escaping.** *(Award 1 mark for 'One Ear'. Award 2 marks for 'One Ear' supported by evidence from the text. Award 3 marks for 'One Ear' supported by evidence from the text and an explanation demonstrating how they are connected. Maximum 3 marks.)*

5. **Yes, because they say that the wolves 'know' they aren't 'loaded to kill', which suggests they are worried that they are defenceless. They are also watching the wolves getting closer every night and think they should be 'more respectful'. or No, because they 'amused themselves' by trying to spot the wolves in the darkness. They are treating it like a game.** *(Award 1 mark for 'Yes' or 'No' with a reason not closely connected to the text. Award 2 marks for 'Yes' or 'No' supported by evidence from the text or a reason connected to the text. Award 3 marks for 'Yes' or 'No' supported by evidence from the text and an explanation demonstrating how they are connected. Maximum 3 marks.)*

Answers

Comprehension practice page 1

(page 95) continued

6. **'whispered'. It emphasises that they were scared/cautious. or 'crackled'/'spluttering'. It heightens the tension as the fire gains strength.** *(Award 1 mark for the example of onomatopoeia. Award 2 marks for the example of onomatopoeia and a general explanation of onomatopoeia. Award 3 marks for the example of onomatopoeia and a specific explanation of how the example picked affects the reader. Maximum 3 marks.)*

7. **She is the 'decoy' for the pack. This means that she lures a dog out from the human's pack and then the rest of the wolf pack come and eat it.** *(Award 1 mark for 'decoy'. Award 2 marks for 'decoy' and the explanation that she lures the dogs out. Award 3 marks for 'decoy' and the explanation that she lures the dogs out so that they can be attacked/eaten by the other wolves. Maximum 3 marks.)*

8. **i) One Ear**
   ii) length/eagerness
   iii) strained/whined
   iv) full

   (Award 1 mark for each correct answer. Maximum 4 marks.)

Comprehension practice page 2 (page 96)

1. **Mary is brave because it says she is not 'timid'. She is independent because she does 'what she wanted'. She is also curious/adventurous because she looks for the 'mysterious garden'.** *(Award 1 mark for an impression based on the correct part of the text. Award 2 marks for an impression with evidence from the correct part of the text. Award 3 marks for two impressions with evidence from the correct part of the text. Maximum 3 marks.)*

2. **She wanted that door to be the one leading to the mysterious garden.**

3. **a collection of fruit-bearing trees.**

4. **unpleasant/miserable/scowling**

5. **The author uses rhetorical questions (for example, 'Why had Mr Archibald Craven buried the key?') to make the reader think about the mysteries connected to the garden. or The author says that Mary is 'curious'/'thought so much' about the garden, which makes it sound interesting and mysterious. or The author calls it 'deserted', which makes it sound like there is a mystery connected to it. Gardens are not usually deserted, so the reader wants to find out why this one is.** *(Award 1 mark for one point. Award 2 marks for one point with supporting evidence. Award 3 marks for one point with supporting evidence and an explanation demonstrating how they are connected. Maximum 3 marks.)*

Comprehension practice page 3

(pages 97–98)

1. **B**   3. **B**   5. **B**   7. **D**   9. **C**
2. **C**   4. **A**   6. **C**   8. **D**   10. **D**

Comprehension practice page 4 (page 99)

1. **'The moon has a face like the clock in the hall' is a simile. It is effective because a clock is round and high up in the hall just like the moon is round and high up in the night sky.** *(Award 1 mark for 'simile'. Award 2 marks for 'simile' and a general explanation of similes. Award 3 marks for 'simile' and a specific explanation of how the example picked affects the reader. Maximum 3 marks.)*

2. **A fork in a tree is the point where two branches meet and jut out like the prongs of a fork.**

3. **The cat is making a squalling sound, which is loud, whereas the mouse is squeaking, which is quiet.** *(Award 1 mark for identifying the noises the cat and mouse are making. Award 2 marks for identifying the noises and explaining the difference between them. Maximum 2 marks.)*

4. *Examples of personification could include:*
   'The bat that lies in bed at noon'/'All of the things ... cuddle to sleep'/'And flowers ... close their eyes'.
   By giving human qualities to non-human things, the poet can contrast when different animals, people and things are awake and asleep. *(Award 1 mark for the example of personification. Award 2 marks for the example of personification and a general explanation of personification. Award 3 marks for the example of personification and a specific explanation of how the example picked affects the reader. Maximum 3 marks.)*

5. **The general atmosphere is calm, peaceful and relaxing because of the repetitive rhythm of the poem, the long vowel sounds and the rhyme (for example, 'hall' and 'wall'). The only noises that interrupt the calm mood in the poem are the 'squalling cat', the 'squeaking mouse' and the 'howling dog'.** *(Award 1 mark for a point about the atmosphere. Award 2 marks for a point about the atmosphere supported by evidence from the text. Award 3 marks for a point about the atmosphere supported by evidence from the text and an explanation demonstrating how the evidence supports the point. Maximum 3 marks.)*

6. **AABB/pair of consecutive rhyming words/ the first and second lines rhyme in each verse, and the third and fourth lines rhyme in each verse. It creates a calm, gentle rhythm and effect/makes the reader feel calm/sleepy.** *(Award 1 mark for a partial description of the rhyme scheme. Award 2 marks for a full description of the rhyme scheme. Award 3 marks for a full description of the rhyme scheme and a description of its effect on the reader. Maximum 3 marks.)*

Schofield & Sims

Answers

Writing

In this section, answers are only sample answers and children's answers may vary considerably. Where sample answers are given, use the writing rubric on page 119 as a general guide as well as considering any specific points mentioned in the sample answers.

Planning narrative writing (page 110)

1. Introduction: late for school – pressed snooze.

   Build up: ran to station – queue – 'snaking round the station'. Electrical fault – 'heart sank like a stone; panic ... like lava bubbling'.

   Climax: dialogue with ticket inspector, remember emotional responses.

   Resolution: saved by travel news, relief!

   Conclusion: get to school – thank Mum, reflections. Short sentences – look ahead to new challenge.

2. Introduction: precious statue – family heirloom. Describe it. Can't touch.

   Build up: describe weather. Boredom/frustration – can't go outside. Mum shopping – indoor football with brother.

   Climax: brother whacks ball. Hits statue – 'breaks into a million pieces'. Describe fright, heart beating.

   Resolution: collect pieces – will glue work? Use dialogue – blame.

   Conclusion: sounds of car/footsteps/door. Describe feelings of dread. 'Now we were in for it! We gulped.'

3. Introduction: moved house – describe lots of boxes/bags/furniture everywhere. Excited – bigger than old house – explore.

   Build up: open every door – describe some rooms. Find locked door. Describe curiosity. Use rhetorical questions.

   Climax: scratching noises behind door. Startled and worried – what could it be? Getting louder and louder. Hear strange howling noise. Monster?

   Resolution: run to find Mum – she gets ring of keys. Try every key but none fit. Break the door down. Red flash dashes past – a fox!

   Conclusion: wonder how long it had been in there and why the door was locked. Relief – laugh – no monsters, but also no door now!

4. Introduction: present day – lying in hospital, staring at walls. Why had I been so foolish?

   Build up: describe abandoned house. Told it was dangerous. Light on – dared to go in. Describe inside – crumbling ceiling, flaking walls, cobwebs.

   Climax: final dare – go upstairs. Creaky, dusty, banisters full of splinters. Shout 'I'm the king of the world!' at top. Banister breaks away from the stairs – tumble down. Describe emotions and pain.

Resolution: brother screams/cries in fright. Builders with torches rush over and call ambulance.

Conclusion: in hospital/present. Leg in plaster – can't move. Builder and Mum by bed, check I'm OK and warn me never to enter derelict houses again!

5. Introduction: important maths test – worried about fractions. Reassurance from teacher.

   Build up: revision difficult – simile 'fractions disperse on the page like confetti' – go to teacher at lunch to ask for help.

   Climax: waiting outside the classroom, hear voices from the cupboard, "She'll never know. Take it home and learn it." Friends have copy of maths test. Rhetorical questions – tell on them? Ask for copy?

   Resolution: friends come out and see me. Want to know if I heard – say no. Don't believe me – they'll know who it was if they get in trouble. Describe fear but also wish to do the right thing.

   Conclusion: they run off. I'm sweating. What to do? Teacher opens door – cliffhanger ending.

6. Introduction: friends with next-door neighbour. Describe memories. Parents crashed their cars and argued – can't play together any more.

   Build up: begged parents to change mind – 'but they were adamant'. Describe emotions (sadness, frustration). Had to find a way to meet.

   Climax: my plan – secret messages through gap in fence. First message – soggy/ink smudged in rain. Second message – bird stole for nest. Describe sadness.

   Resolution: next day – sun shining – reflection. Investigate – perfume bottle – describe smell. Paper inside – 'Meet me tomorrow after school by the bus stop.' – friend had same idea!

   Conclusion: describe emotions – use exclamations. Meet up with friend – 'Our parents' feud would not thwart our friendship!'

Planning descriptive writing (page 111)

1. Introduction: hot, sunny, lazy afternoon. Setting – the park. Everyone sat under trees to avoid the burning heat. Blankets stretched out, spread of delicious food.

   Detail 1: describe the blanket full of food. Develop smell, taste and texture as well as sights. Describe reactions of family as they eat the food. Add detail of dog trying to steal the food.

   Detail 2: the setting – park. Trees (branches, leaves, swaying in the wind), pond – people feeding ducks. Soft grass to sit on.

   Detail 3: weather – white fluffy clouds, turquoise sky, gentle warm breeze, warming sun beating down.

   Conclusion: time to go – everyone packs up the food, catches the rubbish that the dog has grabbed, shake the crumbs for the pigeons.

Answers

Planning descriptive writing

(page 111) continued

2. Introduction: summer holidays, crowded beach, umbrellas everywhere, can't see the sand for all the beach towels.

   Detail 1: sea – gentle waves rippling, crystal clear, reflecting the sun's shimmering rays, tiny fish darting and avoiding the bathers.

   Detail 2: people – children and dogs scampering around, splashing through the sea, building sandcastles, giggling together. Parents relaxing.

   Detail 3: seagulls – snow white feathers soaring through the air, their beady eyes snooping for scraps of food. Sharp beaks snapping at anything thrown or dropped on the floor. Use imagery.

   Conclusion: after a long, busy day, people start to leave. Umbrellas get dismantled, chairs get folded away. 'The soft silky sand can be seen once again, and all is still and quiet as the sun starts to set.'

3. Introduction: French teacher. Background – name, how long she taught me for.

   Detail 1: appearance and personality – kind eyes, smiling face, long curly hair tied with bright hair bands.

   Detail 2: her teaching style – fun as she used to play lots of games and do role play (give example of shopping), she always explained difficult concepts well (such as verb tenses) and was so passionate.

   Detail 3: why she was inspiring – she expressed the importance of being able to speak someone else's language. She made France sound exciting – the museums, the landscape, the food.

   Conclusion: still speak and learn French; want to learn more words and visit lots of places in France because of my special teacher.

4. Introduction: afternoon on a cool, autumnal day. Sun setting, 'sending long low golden rays through the branches of the trees'.

   Detail 1: the trees – crimson red, mustard yellow. Personification of leaves – 'saying goodbye to the branches who have held them tightly through the summer'; 'dancing and twirling to the ground'.

   Detail 2: the animals – squirrels scurrying to collect acorns, busy digging and hiding them in the ground. Hedgehogs scuttling to find a safe place to sleep, collecting leaves to make a warm bed for winter.

   Detail 3: people – walking through forest, crunching leaves on the ground, collecting shiny conkers, flinging leaves into the air.

   Conclusion: the sun has set, darkness prevails, the air cools further, the leaves seem darker not glowing. The soft hoot of owls can be heard as night falls.

5. Introduction: busy Saturday morning at the Natural History Museum. Excited children waiting outside. Manager opens the door. Tall, imposing doors creak open to reveal a wealth of treasures.

   Detail 1: the hall. Gargantuan whale skeleton suspended from ceiling. Simile – long backbone like a snake stretching across the hall.

   Detail 2: dinosaur room – gigantic skeletons of these lizard monsters dominate the room. They are standing, ready to pounce. Pterodactyls swoop above, ready to plunge to grab unsuspecting prey.

   Detail 3: the Neanderthal room – a gloomy cave with models of cavemen building a fire to keep warm and cook. Their stooped bodies are muscular and hairy. Long wiry beards and leathery skin.

   Conclusion: so many more rooms to visit – jungle, arctic, desert. Can't wait to explore!

6. Introduction: set the scene – my 10th birthday. Special – double-digits. Party in full swing.

   Detail 1: the decorations – brightly coloured balloons bob and dangle from the ceiling. Snake-like streamers stretch across the ceiling – use metaphor 'shiny spaghetti'. Huge banner – 'Happy 10th birthday'.

   Detail 2: a table with a mountain of food – sweet sticky doughnuts iced with a shiny, glistening coating; huge birthday cake covered in multi-coloured sprinkles and chocolate flakes; a chocolate fountain flowing with a glossy brown river of chocolate and fluffy, puffy marshmallows waiting to dive in and be smothered.

   Detail 3: the people – smiling grandmothers, my frazzled parents trying to keep the place tidy, friends and cousins laughing and playing party games.

   Conclusion: reflecting on what a lovely day it was – everybody smiling and laughing. Describe emotions.

Planning non-fiction writing (page 113)

1. Introduction: addresses, 'Dear Ms Hall', explain why I'm writing.

   Reason 1: gives pupils a chance to express themselves. They spend all week looking the same so could be an opportunity to be creative.

   Reason 2: could be used as a reward – only people who keep the uniform rules all week get to wear their own clothes on Friday.

   Reason 3: could be used to raise money. People donate a small amount each week for the privilege. Money goes to good causes including the school.

   Conclusion: I hope you find my arguments compelling. Please consider and discuss with staff. 'Yours sincerely'.

2. Introduction: we've all seen the horrendous images on TV and in the news – ice caps melting, starving polar bears, flooding. Down to global warming that we have contributed to. We can do something about it.

   Solution 1: car emissions cause greenhouse gases. Reduce number of trips by car. Walk, car share, cycle.

   Solution 2: reduce the amount of plastic we use whose manufacture causes greenhouse gases. Reuse plastic bags, drink from reusable cups and bottles.

Schofield & Sims

Solution 3: eat less meat – cows produce a lot of methane which is a greenhouse gas. Reduce the demand for meat so fewer cows will be bred and less methane will be produced.

Conclusion: if we all change our lifestyle habits, we can reduce greenhouse emissions and slow down global warming. What are you waiting for?

3. Headline and introduction (lead sentence): New Leisure Centre Makes a Splash!

'Yesterday afternoon, the new Waterfall Leisure Centre finally opened to the public after five years of development.'

Point 1: huge crowd, really pleased – under construction for so long. Area hasn't had a swimming pool since previous leisure centre closed.

Point 2: new leisure centre has two pools, gym, sports hall, squash courts and outdoor play area. Will also host children's birthday parties.

Point 3: will benefit everyone in local area – fitter and healthier. Partner with local schools to provide education and lessons.

Quote: pupil in crowd "I can't wait to start my swimming lessons next week!"

Conclusion: special deal this weekend – half price. Fun for all the family. Come on down!

4. Introduction: exclamation – 'What a strange experience I had at the park!' Poisonous snake escaped from pet shop.

Paragraph 2: picnic with Sasha on her birthday. Lovely summer's day. What could go wrong?

Paragraph 3: describe noises in tree above – squirrels were squealing and birds were squawking. Lots of rustling. Then I saw the snake – long, slippery and scaly, beady eye, forked tongue, hissing.

Paragraph 4: scream – describe emotions. Park keepers come to help. They used specialist equipment including a retractable hook to coax the snake into a box to return him safely to the shop. Background to his disappearance.

Conclusion: we finished our picnic next to the pond – under no trees! Perhaps next time, we will look up and check the tree for snakes before we sit under it!

5. Introduction: state place, date, time. Explain that I'm upset and why – birthday, looking forward to it.

Detail 1: lack of availability of items – had to order third choice. Made me feel disappointed.

Detail 2: food arrived cold. Hair on food. Sauce was missing. These issues weren't ever fixed.

Detail 3: no-one to complain to. Server said manager was busy and head chef refused to leave kitchen. No-one provided compensation or an apology.

Conclusion: I hope you can understand our concerns. Want full refund and your promise that we never have such a dreadful experience ever again. Use emotive language.

6. Introduction: 'Dear diary'. Exciting day – bet you can't guess what happened!

Paragraph 2: describe being woken up when Dad called 'Mary Anning!'. Breakfast with brother.

Paragraph 3: describe beautiful weather – perfect for fossil hunting! Go down to coast together.

Paragraph 4: search the rocks for hours. Describe all the different sorts of fossils found with brother. Use similes.

Conclusion: what a wonderful day! Found lots of fossils to sell in our shop. Can't wait to find more.

Improving your writing (pages 114–118)

1. He could feel the anger coursing through his veins. It was as if steam was billowing out of his ears, and his cheeks turned a beetroot red. Glaring eyes stared at me in fury. I crumbled in front of him as I felt his wrath emanating from his whole body.

2. Slowly, the blazing beams of sunlight grew paler and weaker. The temperature dropped and a chill breeze flowed through the air. A heavy cloak of black cloud swept across the sky like a jaguar stalking through the grass. There was something in the air that suggested rain was on its way.

3. Ferociously, the angry wind whipped up the sea, creating snow-white froth and foam. The sea was like an angry monster, writhing and wriggling in anger. Precariously, the boat tipped from side to side, a juggling ball in careless hands. Thunder roared and lightning flashed in fury.

4. Sewing and knitting are excellent hobbies for developing fine motor skills. Having to work so carefully with a sewing or knitting needle requires a huge amount of dexterity in your fingers. It's amazing how nimble your fingers will become with the hours of practice these skills require. This dexterity will assist you with other hobbies, such as painting or playing a musical instrument.

5. Stealthily, the cat crawled towards the unsuspecting bird, which was happily pecking at the seeds in the grass. With widened eyes and keen focus, the cat had the target in his sights. His whiskers twitched in anticipation as he launched his attack on the terrified bird. Thankfully, with one flap of its wings, it managed to escape from the razor-sharp clutches of the ravenous beast.

6. A few light flakes of snow settled on Norah's coat. She watched them melt into the fabric, then looked back at her phone. Her heart sank: there was still no signal. Straining further, she stretched up as far as she could, teetering right on the edge of the rocky platform they had found refuge on.

"Careful, Norah!" Rick called weakly. He was still clutching at his ankle and there was no chance he was walking back down the mountain. What were they going to do if she couldn't call for help?

Answers

Improving your writing

(pages 114–118) continued

7. Large snowflakes cascaded from the sky.

8. She stormed in and slammed the door.

9. I am shocked and appalled at how many helpless, distraught people are left alone at Christmas.

10. I would be ecstatic if you could donate money to this compassionate, worthy charity.

11. Coloured flags fluttered in the wind like wings on a bird.

12. Puffs of cloud wafted across the sky like spun candyfloss.

13. Bright yellow flowers smiled at the sun as they were warmed by its comforting rays.

14. Lightning spread its electric fingers across the sky in fury.

15. That door seems to be locked, but there is no keyhole.

    What do you think is behind that door?

    How strange it is that the door has never been opened!

    Go and find help to get this door open.

16. Those two children don't have the same opinion as each other.

    Why are those children disagreeing with one another?

    What a pity it is that these children aren't listening to each other!

    Tell the teacher that these children are upset.

17. The town centre is packed with the Saturday market.

    "How much for a bag of potatoes?"

    "What a good deal that is!"

    "Buy one get one free!"

18. The regatta takes place every year.

    "Can you save me a seat?"

    "How strong the wind is today!"

    "Go faster!"

19. Thousands of gallons of poisonous smoke are emitted from that factory every day.

    Do you know how many noxious fumes are in the poisonous gas billowing from that chimney?

    What a difference it makes to breathe clean air!

    Imagine what that smoke must be doing to our lungs.

20. Children will become confident swimmers if they learn to swim before they are five years old.

    Why would we delay when this policy offers so many wonderful benefits?

    How amazing it is to see young children swimming with such agility!

    Think of all the wonderful activities and sports they will be able to do.

21. The fish swam away from the ravenous shark with razor-sharp teeth.

22. With great ferocity, the bear chased the hunters.

23. After a concerted effort from the keepers, the crocodile is now safely back in his enclosure.

24. Scratch! There it was again. My heart pounded. I had to investigate.

25. Imagine. Poor lonely creatures. Shut away in the dark. Helpless and hopeless.

26. The footsteps got louder. I panicked. I started to run. They followed.

27. I Flitting above the turrets, small black bats found their way home to roost.

    C Though it was dark, I could just make out shadowy shapes moving in the dim room.

    E Terrified, I tiptoed up to the door of the old, abandoned house on the hill.

    A Intricate, sticky cobwebs hung from the corners of every room.

    S As cold as ice, the groaning wind whipped through the shivering trees.

    A Mysteriously, faint lights flickered on and off throughout the night.

    P Deep in the cellar, small creatures scuttled along the dusty, stone floor.

28. I Waving their arms like flags, Sunita and Peter whizzed round the track in their carriage.

    C Despite their crippling fear, Arif and Yuchen were determined to keep their eyes open.

    E Excited and exhilarated, Josh and Precious screamed and wailed in delight.

    A Ear-piercing screeches from the death-defying roller coaster echoed around the whole park.

    S Like a pack of hyenas, Sanjay and Li laughed and giggled their way around the twists and turns of the ride.

    A Tenaciously, Melanie clung to the safety bar, fearing she might be flung out like a slingshot.

    P From high above, the roller coaster plunged like a stone towards the ground.

29. I Feeling pressured, parents often submit to the pleas of their children for more screen time.

    C If we allow this shocking trend to continue, children will spend less time interacting with their peers.

    E Concerned by these findings, doctors are making new recommendations for what is an acceptable amount of screen time for children.

    A Blurry vision and poor focus are two symptoms of spending too much time in front of a screen.

    S As entrancing as a hypnotist, the lure of screens is too great for children to resist.

    A Surprisingly, children as young as two years old are spending more than an hour a day on a phone.

P During one evening, a child can clock up a staggering three to four hours staring at a screen.

30. She could feel something strange happening – the ground was crumbling beneath her!

31. In the distance, smoke was rising – she sensed that something wasn't right.

32. The use of the library at lunchtime is invaluable to Year 6 pupils – especially before exams.

33. Everyone stood up and cheered; she'd finally achieved her dream of winning a gold medal.

34. She felt much better; after a few minutes of fresh air, she was able to get back in the car.

35. Hunting animals with dogs is cruel and violent: they suffer a lengthy, excruciating death.

Writing practice page 1 (page 120)

1. *A newspaper report should contain: an appropriate headline; an introductory paragraph setting the scene; chronological details of what happened; emotive and dramatic language; quotes from an eyewitness; a closing paragraph detailing what will happen next or summarising the feelings now.*

2. *The story should continue with an appropriately mysterious or eerie atmosphere. It should contain the characters Danny and Clare, spelt correctly, and be written in the third person. The cause of the rustling could be revealed. The characters should be referring to getting back to camp.*

3. *A diary should start with an appropriate greeting such as 'Dear diary'. The events should be described in order with some detailed description and emotions and reactions. The events should all be based around a boat trip upon which something surprising happens. It should be written from the writer's point of view. The events should be recounted in the past tense. There should be a closing summary of how they are feeling now and what they have learnt or hope will happen next.*

4. *The format should resemble a letter with the address, date and greeting. The letter should be written with a formal style, avoiding contractions and any colloquial language. There should be an appropriate opening that explains why they are writing and provides some context. There should be separate paragraphs detailing ideas for addressing the issue. There should be an appropriate conclusion asking for the councillor's response.*

5. *There should be an appropriate introduction introducing what happened. There should be a dramatic recount of the event with appropriate description (of the animal in particular), and emotions and reactions. There should be an appropriate reflection at the end.*

6. *The format should resemble a letter with the address, date and greeting. There should be an appropriate introduction that sets the context and explains why they are writing. Approximately three paragraphs*

should follow giving relevant details and the child's emotions and reactions to them. The child should be able to include relevant historical information from the era. The letter should end with a conclusion, explaining what they'd like to happen next and asking for a response.

7. *The opening paragraph should address the audience and introduce why they are speaking. Detailed paragraphs should follow explaining the changes with the benefits, using persuasive techniques, such as rhetorical questions and use of the second person. The final paragraph should ask for a response.*

8. *A general paragraph should be included setting the scene and creating the appropriate atmosphere as decided by the child. Various paragraphs should follow describing an aspect of the picture in more detail using a range of imagery and figurative language. A final paragraph should close the scene, perhaps with a change of time or mood.*

Writing practice page 2 (page 121)

1. *The format should resemble a letter with the address, date and greeting. There should be an appropriate introduction, explaining why they are writing and setting the context. There should be three or four subsequent paragraphs detailing different points that the reader should consider about the new school, with guidance on how to approach each situation. It should have a friendly, semi-formal tone, but avoid colloquialisms, and address the reader directly. A final paragraph should include a general feeling of reassurance and excitement about meeting the new pupil.*

2. *The continuation should link to the passage and contain some plot whereby Toad gets involved in a problem with the car he has stolen. It should address his mischievous nature and probably end with a climax containing an accident, his capture or some other event that stops him keeping the car. A range of reactions from himself or other people is required along with detailed descriptions of what happens and accompanying speech to suggest reactions.*

3. *A diary should start with an appropriate greeting such as 'Dear diary'. The events should be described in order with some detailed description and emotions and reactions. The events should all be based around a specific fear and how the writer conquered it. It should be written from the writer's point of view. The events should be recounted in the past tense. There should be a closing summary of how they are feeling now and what they have learnt or hope will happen next.*

4. *The story should have an appropriate introduction setting the scene. It should build to a climax whereby the theme of the lost key is explored in detail. A resolution could resolve the problem of the missing key or leave it on a cliffhanger. There should be a conclusion thinking about what the characters feel now and perhaps what they have learnt.*

Answers

Writing practice page 2 (page 121) continued

5. The newspaper article should begin with an appropriate headline and an introductory paragraph setting the scene. It should include examples of how computer games cause problems with reactions to those; emotive and dramatic language; and quotes from people involved on both sides of the issue. It may also include opinions and solutions from the writer. The article should end with a closing paragraph summarising the feelings of people in the present and perhaps suggesting improvements for the future.

Writing practice page 3 (page 122)

1. i) A diary should start with an appropriate greeting such as 'Dear diary'. The events should be described in order with some detailed description and emotions and reactions. The events should all be based around details from the passage read with appropriate imagined subsequent events. It should be written from the writer's point of view. The events should be recounted in the past tense. There should be a closing summary of how they are feeling now and what they have learnt or hope will happen next.

ii) The letter should be written in an informal, friendly style. There should be an appropriate opening, explaining why they are writing with some context based on the passage read. There should be separate paragraphs detailing the events in order with appropriate emotions and reactions. There should be an appropriate conclusion about what is going to happen next.

iii) A newspaper report should begin with an appropriate headline and an introductory paragraph setting the scene. It should include chronological details of what happened detailing events from the passage, emotive and dramatic language and quotes from people who may know Chris Hadfield. The article should end with a closing paragraph summarising the feelings in the town now and detailing what will happen next.

iv) The format should resemble a letter with the address, date and greeting. There should be an appropriate introduction, explaining why they are writing and setting the context. There should be three or four paragraphs detailing points that the reader wants to share about their feelings towards Chris Hadfield with appropriate questions to ask as well. It should have a semi-formal, respectful tone but still avoid colloquialisms. The letter should address the reader directly. A final paragraph should include a general feeling of admiration towards Chris Hadfield, with perhaps a request for a response.

v) The letter should be written with a formal style, avoiding contractions and any colloquial language. There should be an appropriate opening, explaining why they are writing with some context provided about wishing to join the scholarship scheme.

There should be separate paragraphs detailing ideas for addressing the writer's suitability for the scheme, using persuasive features as appropriate. There should be an appropriate conclusion asking for the recipient's response.

Practice test (pages 124–133)

All questions are worth 1 mark for a correct answer except where marking guidance alongside answers indicates how multiple marks can be earnt. Answers must be fully correct to earn credit on a 1 mark question.

Sentences, phrases and clauses

1. phrase

2. subordinate clause

3. main clause

4. complex sentence

Paragraphs

5. Michelle Obama is a former First Lady of the United States and the wife of the 44th president, Barack Obama. She was also the first African American First Lady. **/** Obama was born in Chicago on 17th January 1964. Having studied hard at school, she then attended Princeton University and Harvard Law School, after which she began a career in law. **/** Michelle met Barack Obama at work. They got married in 1992 and have two daughters. (*Award 1 mark for each paragraph symbol. Maximum 2 marks.*)

Nouns

6.

Common noun	bees
Proper noun	Daniel
Collective noun	swarm
Abstract noun	courage

(*Award 1 mark for each noun. Maximum 4 marks.*)

Pronouns

7. The Wallace family enjoy playing games. **They** particularly enjoy bridge, although Fabian, the oldest brother, always wins, whoever **his** partner is. **He** is exceptionally competitive, and **he** always makes sure **they** follow the rules meticulously. (*Award 1 mark for 'the Wallace family' replaced with the correct pronoun each time. Award 1 mark for 'Fabian' replaced with the correct pronoun each time. Maximum 2 marks.*)

8. Sophie was so pleased with *themselves* / **herself** / *ourselves* for passing her music exam that she told all **her** / *his* / *hers* friends immediately. (*Award 1 mark for one correct answer underlined. Award 2 marks for both correct answers underlined. Maximum 2 marks.*)

Verbs

9. As I **drew** the curtains, I **noticed** it **was** a beautiful sunny day.

10. In the future, I **hope** that we **will slow** the rate of global warming.

11. **past tense**

12. Every Tuesday, I **gone** to classes at the youth centre. **go**

13. Next week, my sister will **took** a very important driving test. **take**

Active and passive sentences

14. **passive**

15. **The map that I needed was taken out of my old, blue rucksack by Frankie.**

Prepositions

16. **In** the night, a huge volume of snow fell. **time**

17. i) **After** a long drive, we arrived **at** the hotel.

ii) **During** winter, animals hibernate to escape the cold conditions.

iii) The diver swam far **below** her normal depth.

iv) I walked **around** the hole in the pavement.

Adjectives

18. **superlative**　　**19.** **positive adjective**

Adverbs

20. The weather is **extremely** chilly today so I will need to wrap up **warmly**.

21. I am eating a **very** large piece of chocolate cake which was cooked **yesterday** by my brother.

22. While Ty tried to sleep, loud thunder roared **deafeningly** and blinding bolts of lightning flashed **brilliantly**.

Connectives

23. We would like to inform you that, **although** this evening's performance of *Cinderella* is fully booked, we can offer you a seat in the mayor's box. This is a special honour **as** nobody else has been offered this privilege. **However**, the mayor was particularly impressed with all the charity work you do, **so** she suggested you be given this opportunity. **If** you would like to book the seat, please contact the box office immediately. (*Award 1 mark for three or more connectives underlined. Award 2 marks for all five connectives underlined. Maximum 2 marks.*)

24. *While* / *Through* / *Despite* the film was running, the projector stopped working.

25. That milk will go sour *if* / *for* / **unless** you put it in the fridge.

26. I will bring the washing in from the garden **in case** / *because* / *and* it starts to rain.

Determiners

27. "Leave **that** box alone – it's **her** special present," said Annis.

28. **Several** bakers have exclaimed that **this** banana bread tastes wonderful.

29. Have you saved **enough** money to buy **the** jumper you like?

Sentence punctuation

30. ⓦhat a strange day I've had Ⓐs I was walking to school with Zainah, what do you think I saⓦ Ⓞut of nowhere, hailstones started falling. ⓣhey weren't normal hailstones though – they were as big as Christmas puddings. We ran inside quickly. ⓘ wonder where they came fromⓟ

*W*hat a strange day I've had*!* As I was walking to school with Zainah, what do you think I saw*?* Out of nowhere, hailstones started falling. *T*hey weren't normal hailstones though – they were as big as Christmas puddings. We ran inside quickly. *I* wonder where they came from **...** (or **.**) (*Award 1 mark for two or more punctuation mistakes circled. Award 2 marks for four or more punctuation mistakes circled. Award 3 marks for all six punctuation mistakes circled. Maximum 3 marks.*)

31. **C**

Commas

32. "Ifⓒ you're going to the shop please get me some milkⓒ Josie called out to Freya. Her list was already massive: bread, cheeseⓒeggs, pasta and sauce, cereal, bananasⓒand apples. She went back inside to get a bigger bag, but she nearly forgot her purse! (*Award 1 mark for two incorrect or missing commas circled. Award 2 marks for three incorrect or missing commas circled. Award 3 marks for all four incorrect or missing commas circled with no mistakes. Maximum 3 marks.*)

Brackets and dashes

33. Lebkuchen **(**a type of German biscuit**)** are often eaten at Christmas.

34. The letter **–** the one I sent last week **–** has not been delivered yet.

35. It was the perfect result **–** she won by a mile.

36. West Sussex **(**a county in England) is located on the south coast.

Colons and semicolons

37. I missed Saran's 12th birthday party**:** I was ill.

38. On Saturday, Femi went to football practice**;** Jake stayed at home and watched a film.

Answers

Hyphens

39. Our much-loved teacher retired at the age of sixty-seven.

Apostrophes

40. Marcus' dog couldn't find its favourite ball in the park, so Marcus asked the other owners if their dogs might've taken it. (*Award 1 mark for two correct apostrophes. Award 2 marks for all three correct apostrophes. Maximum 2 marks.*)

Speech marks

41. "Have you seen that new movie set on Mars?" asked Jensen. "I thought it was really good." The other children smiled in agreement, except for Dylan.

"Perhaps," he started, "it would have been better if there were fewer CGI effects." Some people nodded, yet others shook their heads.

Yi commented that he liked how real the aliens looked. "They scared me half to death!" he added. (*Award 1 mark for speech punctuation and line breaks partially correct. Award 2 marks for speech punctuation and line breaks mostly correct. Award 3 marks for all speech punctuation and line breaks correct. Maximum 3 marks.*)

Direct speech and reported speech

42. **Jessica asked if that was the page she needed to complete her answers on.**

43. **"When does the match start?" said Max. "I hope my team wins."**

Singular and plural words

44. Elegantly, the *deers* / **deer** / *deeres* trotted across the path.

45. I always cut my **sandwiches** / *sandwich's* / *sandwitchis* into triangles.

46. **wolves**

47. **families**

Root words, prefixes and suffixes

48. It is **inpolite** to start eating while everyone else is still waiting for their meal to be delivered. **impolite**

49. Many people try to disprove the moon landing, but I think they are **disled**. **misled**

50. **inconvenience**

51. **easily**

52. **expect**

53. **proper**

Homophones

54. **vain**

55. **complimentary**

56. He was given an eighteen *carrot* / **carat** gold ring but he **knew** / *new* it wouldn't fit.

57. The **stationery** / *stationary* cupboard was full of *grate* / **great** resources.

Spot spelling mistakes

58. It was **necesary** to redecorate the disgusting room. **necessary**

59. Eva was **desparate** to win the important match. **desperate**

60. He was a very **mischievous** / *mischievious* / *mischiefous* dog.

Synonyms and antonyms

61. **dampness**

62. **margin**

63. **tempestuous**

64. **disappear**

65. i) **perplexed, bewildered, bemused**
(*Award 1 mark for each synonym. Maximum 3 marks.*)

ii) **opulent, luxurious, lavish**
(*Award 1 mark for each antonym. Maximum 3 marks*)

66. **astute**

67. **interior**

68. **meagre**

69. **indolent**

70. i) **participate**

ii) **extravagant**

Homonyms

71. **match**

72. **current**

73. **address**

74. **bark**

Cloze

75. In the **early** years of the US space programme, the National Advisory **Committee** for Aeronautics (NACA) did not have machines to do their calculations. Instead, they relied on **human** mathematicians, who were called computers. Dorothy Vaughan joined the NACA as a human computer and was promoted to be the **supervisor** of the West Area Computing unit in 1949. She was the first African American **woman** to take this **role**.

When the NACA turned into NASA around a decade **later**, electronic computers were **replacing** human computers. Vaughan joined NASA and learnt the **programming** language FORTRAN. She was a **successful** computer programmer until she retired in 1971. (*Award 1 mark for each correctly placed word. Maximum 10 marks.*)

Schofield & Sims

Abbreviations, acronyms and initialisms

76. initialism

77. acronym

78. compact disk

79. department

Compound words

80. (bat **ball** bored) (**room** bath hit) (ballroom)

81. (see me **no**) (ate went **on**) (noon)

82. out (outgrow, outfit, outlaw, outwit)

83. bed (bedroom, bedsheet, bedstead, bedtime)

Comprehension

84. i) The music sounded so sweet/beautiful.

ii) a window

iii) Yes, because the Giant says 'at last' like he has been looking forward to the Spring. He also 'jumped' out of bed when he thought the Spring had arrived. (*Award 1 mark for the answer 'Yes' and a plausible reason. Award 2 marks for the answer 'Yes' and a plausible reason supported by evidence from the text. Maximum 2 marks.*)

iv) The word arms refers to the tree's branches. The personification makes it easier for you to imagine what the branches look like and how they move in the wind. (*Award 1 mark for reference to the tree's branches. Award 2 marks for reference to the tree's branches and a plausible reason connected to the text. Maximum 2 marks.*)

v) blossoms/flowers

vi) Yes, because the Giant will help the boy get up. I think this because the text says the boy is 'too tiny', but the Giant is big enough to help. or No, because the tree has already 'bent its branches down as low as it could' and the boy is still 'too tiny', so the boy has no way to get up. I think he will give up now. (*Award 1 mark for a prediction and a plausible reason. Award 2 marks for a prediction and a plausible reason supported by evidence from the text. Award 3 marks for a prediction and a plausible reason or reasons supported by detailed explanation or multiple pieces of evidence from the text. Maximum 3 marks.*)

Writing

Marking of these questions should be supported by the guidance given in the Writing mark scheme on page 119. Each question is worth 25 marks.

85. i) *The first paragraph should introduce the setting and the first character. The second and third paragraphs will look at significantly different characters (for example, commuters, tourists, station staff, children, animals). The description will use many of the five senses, vivid details and figurative language where appropriate. The final paragraph will close the scene and show a change in time or mood from the first paragraph.*

ii) *The response to this task will be written from a first-person perspective. It will fulfil the task by providing an account of a single day on a holiday. The first paragraph will introduce the reader to the setting and characters. The second and third paragraphs will provide realistic details that justify the choice of topic. The description will use many of the five senses, vivid details and figurative language where appropriate. The final paragraph will close the scene and provide some reflection on the topic.*

iii) *The response to this task will be set out like a formal letter with addresses and 'Dear' followed by the teacher's name. It should be written in a formal tone without contractions or colloquialisms. The first paragraph will introduce the topic, naming the museum or place of historical interest that has been chosen. It will also sum up the main argument. Subsequent paragraphs will provide details about different aspects of the argument, supported by facts and figures. Persuasive language and figurative language should be included where appropriate. The argument should be summarised briefly in a conclusion, which should also contain a request for a response. The letter should end with 'Yours sincerely' and the writer's name.*

Index and Glossary

abstract noun 9, 10 — the name of anything you can't touch, including feelings and ideas

active voice 17 — when the **subject** does the action of the verb

adverb 22, 23, 29, 33, 55, 87, 118 — a word that describes a verb, an adjective or another **adverb**

affix 51, 54, 65 — both **prefixes** and **suffixes**

alliteration 79, 89, 91, 107 — when several words in a sentence begin with the same sound

analogy 88 — a comparison between two things that are alike in a particular way

antonym 64–68, 74 — a word that means the opposite of another word

auxiliary verb 14–16 — an additional verb used with the main verb to form a tense

clause 5–7, 23, 24, 26, 33–35, 37, 38, 117 — a group of words that includes a verb

cliché 90 — a group of words that has been used lots and is often considered boring

collective noun 9, 10 — the name of a group of things or people

common noun 9, 10 — the name of a type of thing or person

comparative adjective 21 — a word that compares two things

complex sentence 7, 17, 23, 101 — a sentence with one **main clause** and one or more **subordinate clauses**. Any subordinate clauses will begin with a **connective**

compound sentence 7, 23, 101 — a sentence with two **main clauses** that are joined together by a **co-ordinating conjunction**

conjunction 23, 58, 118 — a word or **phrase** that joins other words or parts of sentences together (see also **connective**)

connective 5–7, 23, 24, 29, 33, 119 — a word or **phrase** that joins other words or parts of sentences together (see also **conjunction**)

contraction 11, 40, 41, 55 — a shortened form of one or more words made by leaving some letters out

co-ordinating conjunction 23 — a **connective** that joins two or more **main clauses** (**F**or, **A**nd, **N**or, **B**ut, **O**r, **Y**et, **S**o)

deduce 84 — work something out using other facts that you already know

descriptive writing 100, 101, 105, 106, 111, 116 — a piece of writing that describes a scene without using a plot

determiner 9, 10, 11, 19, 25, 29, 107, 118 — a small word used before a noun to show which one you are referring to (for example, **a, the, one, each**)

dialogue 8, 33, 34, 78, 79, 114, 116 — the words spoken by characters in a book, film or play

direct speech 42–44, 48 — the exact words that a person or character says

ellipsis 31 — punctuation that shows words have been left out or a thought is incomplete

154

Schofield & Sims

Index and Glossary

Index and Glossary

pronoun 9, 11, 12, 19, 21, 27, 41, 44, 55, 90, 101	a word used instead of a noun
proper noun 9, 10, 30, 32, 41, 42, 58	the name of a specific thing or person
prose 78	any writing in ordinary sentences with normal grammar. It is different from **poetry**, which has its own rules
proverb 90	a well-known saying that gives advice on life
reported speech 42–44, 48	when one person or character explains what another person or character has said (see also **indirect speech**)
rhetorical question 80, 90, 113	a question that does not need an answer or can be answered by the person asking the question
rhyme scheme 79	the pattern of words or lines that end with the same sound. Often expressed using a new letter for each repeated sound (for example, **ABAB**)
rhythm 79	a regular pattern of sounds in a poem
root word 39, 51–54, 56, 61	the part of the word that contains the meaning before **prefixes** and **suffixes** are added
scan 16, 82, 92	look through a text quickly to find a particular piece of information
script 37, 43, 79	the written copy of a play or film that shows the **dialogue** and any stage directions
simile 88, 90, 91, 105, 113, 115, 118, 119	a way of describing something by comparing it to something else
simple sentence 7, 101, 116	a sentence with only one **main clause**
skim 82	look at a text quickly to understand the main ideas but not the details
statement 7, 31, 101, 116	a type of sentence that gives information or an opinion
subject 5–7, 11–18, 58, 87, 118, 119	the noun or **pronoun** that does the action in an active sentence
subordinate clause 5, 6, 23, 33, 117	a **clause** that does not make sense by itself. Also known as a dependent clause
subordinating conjunction 23	a **connective** that joins a **main clause** and a **subordinate clause**
suffix 9, 21, 22, 51–54, 56, 59, 61, 64, 66, 86, 87	one or more letters added to the end of a word to change its meaning
superlative adjective 21	a word that compares three or more things
synonym 64–68, 74	a word meaning the same or almost the same as another
verse 79	a group of lines that form one section of a poem. Also known as a stanza
word family 54	words that share the same **root word**

Schofield & Sims